PRAISE FOR
BLAME IT ON JESUS

Don't pick a fight with anybody, even in love, unless Jesus puts you up to it. Jeff and DeDe present Jesus, in all of his risky, loving, belligerence. And they'll show you how to hitch on to what Jesus is up to.
~ Rev. Will Willimon, United Methodist Bishop retired, Professor of the Practice of Christian Ministry, Duke Divinity School, author of Changing My Mind: The Overlooked Virtue for Faithful Ministry.

I've had the privilege of knowing DeDe Jones as both a worship leader and pastor, and she is the real deal. Her voice carries a message of grace that inspires and unites, whether she's singing or speaking. In *Blame it on Jesus*, she and Jeff bring that same passion and authenticity to the page, challenging us to love courageously and live out our faith in transformative ways. DeDe's heart for people shines through in everything she does, and this book is no exception. I've often thought - their message needs to be shared regularly, on a broader, national stage and now, that's happening!
~ Jenny Anchondo, Emmy award-winning news anchor and reporter

DeDe Jones is a powerhouse, both as a worship leader and a writer. She knows how to bring people into God's presence through her voice, and now she brings that same passion to the pages of *Blame it on Jesus.* With Jeff, her co-author and husband, DeDe calls us to a bold, Christ-centered love that moves beyond comfort zones. Their message and ministry are exactly what the church needs today—a wake-up call to live out faith with radical grace and truth.

~ Mike Slaughter, best-selling author and pastor emeritus and global church ambassador for Ginghamsburg Church

DeDe and Jeff Jones' *Blame it on Jesus* is a bold call to love that resonates deeply. Through DeDe's journey, they share a personal perspective on how Jesus' message can foster empathy, justice, and understanding for ALL. This inspiring manifesto invites everyone to embrace the unconditional love of God, which many have been led to believe is closed to them. As someone from the queer community, I've grappled with my faith, but this book helps open the door that others have shut, reminding me that God loves me for who I am. The world desperately needs this message; countless hurting souls need to know that God's love includes them.

~ Shane Jordan, USA Today Best Selling Author

I wholeheartedly endorse *Blame it on Jesus: Seven Lessons for Fighting Back with Love* by DeDe and Jeff Jones. This powerful book offers a refreshing and much-needed perspective on living out Christ's radical love in today's world. The authors beautifully weave personal stories with biblical wisdom that invite readers to embrace the social outcasts

and misfits, face critics gracefully, and use love as an antidote to hate. DeDe and Jeff provide practical guidance for picking our battles wisely while staying true to Jesus' inclusive message. Their authentic voices and pastoral hearts shine through every page, inspiring us to blame our boundless love and acceptance of others on Jesus. This book is a must-read for anyone seeking to embody Christ's transformative love in their daily lives and communities.
~ *Bishop Ruben Saenz Jr., Horizon Texas Conference, The United Methodist Church*

DeDe and Jeff invite us into a world where everyone is valued, accepted, welcomed, and loved by God. If you have ever thought of yourself as a misfit, known a misfit, or perhaps looked upon others as misfits, this book is for you.
~ *Clifton Howard, retired Assistant to the Bishop, Central Texas Conference, The United Methodist Church*

I have witnessed Rev. DeDe Jones' impactful ministry for over thirty years. Today, I am convinced that her most powerful and purposeful work is her advocacy for the love of Jesus and the full inclusion of all people, especially those in the LGBTQ+ community. Through her leadership, she has renewed my hope—not only in the church's role in humanitarian efforts but also in its ability to bring a diverse community together in unity, loving all people into relationship with Jesus Christ.
~ *Randy Austin, Singer and Songwriter*

This book is SO good. From beginning to end, it shows DeDe's spirit and her love for all kinds of people. I was drawn to her when she first came to serve at Lovers Lane nine years ago because of her passion for Jesus—she just loved to sing songs about him all the time! What about the other part we United Methodists like to focus on—what about social change? Then I looked at how she spends her time—pastoring those who find themselves on the margins of society; she doesn't just preach about loving people, she does baptisms, weddings, and funerals for them. She visits them in hospitals. She feeds the homeless with them. She doesn't just talk about being real; she models what it means to have God transform lives. This girl can preach! This girl can sing! This girl is breaking down walls—and this book reflects the best of who she and Jeff are. Read it and expect to be changed.

~ Rev. Donna Whitehead, author of I Am Enough *and Associate Pastor, Lovers Lane UMC*

Rarely does one say something and it is seized by a gifted person and turned into a message that is so impactful. The Reverend DeDe Jones did just that with a post of all things about divisions and the way Jesus would have us act toward others. "Blame It" became a song considered for two Grammy Awards. Then it became a book penned by a very gifted singer and preacher of messages that Jesus' doesn't mind at all getting blamed for. In such a time of division and hate as this, *Blame It on Jesus* is just the word we need to hear and the spirit we need to embrace. "Take it to the cross" is all about where we take our sin and separation from God and God's ways, that's when our Lord and Savior redeems the worst of circumstances with the best of his salvific ways. Read it, absorb it, and live the truth springing forth from this singer, preacher and now, author.

~Rev. Stan Copeland, author and Senior Pastor, Lovers Lane UMC

Lovers Lane Worship

Lovers Lane Worship is the heartbeat of Modern Worship at Lovers Lane United Methodist Church in Dallas, Texas, where the mission is to love ALL people into relationship with Jesus Christ. United by their passion, faith and profound love of music, this team of vocalists, musicians and songwriters shares a message of love, grace and acceptance that transcends the confines of the church walls. Through their harmonies, they seek to uplift spirits and create an environment where ALL people can hear God's message of hope. They are passionate about bringing a fresh look to well-loved songs and creating original music that creates new paths to connect to God. Lovers Lane Worship is more than a name: it's an invitation to experience God's love for ALL with authenticity and joy!

Scan the QR code to discover music or buy merch from Lovers Lane Worship or visit www.llworship.org.

BLAME IT ON JESUS

Seven Lessons for
Fighting Back with Love

DEDE JONES
AND JEFF JONES

For

Stan Copeland

whose words inspired the song

and

Randy Austin and **Rafe Grigar**

who co-wrote with DeDe the song

that inspired this book.

For

The People of Crosswalk

whose love for God

overcomes all barriers

and inspires us to

a deeper faith.

For

Owen

whose potential inspires

our hope for a

brighter, more loving

future.

Contents

INTRODUCTION

WHETHER YOU'RE A CHRISTIAN or not, you've probably heard Jesus get blamed for a whole lot of things. Didn't make it to work on time? "Blame it on Jesus—he wanted me to rest!" Stuck in a long line? "Well, Jesus said patience is a virtue, so I guess he's testing me." The eighteen-year-old dog dies? "Jesus must have needed another puppy angel in heaven." Thank goodness Jesus didn't wear Crocs, or we'd probably try to blame those on him too.

But there's a deeper concern for the topics we see Jesus being blamed for today. Sometimes, whether intentionally or not, we Christians use Jesus' name to make people feel excluded and unwelcome in the church. We become so concerned about our understanding of the "thou shalt and shalt nots" of the Bible, that we forget the foundation of Jesus' message: To first love God, and second love our neighbors as ourselves. As a result, for many people, Christians have become better known for what we stand against than what we stand for.

It's time for us to reclaim Jesus' message. Instead of using his words and other words of scripture to hold people back, we should take a closer look at how Jesus really teaches us to lift people up. Jesus brings a radical message of love for ALL including the outcasts, sinners and those on the margins. It's time for us to stand up for the misfits and fight back with love. When people question our love, that's something we can blame on Jesus.

Maybe you've started feeling uneasy about how the church has rejected people in the name of Jesus. Perhaps you've never felt confident enough to stand up for the loved ones who have faced that rejection. Or maybe you've experienced that rejection yourself and now doubt whether you're worthy to share Jesus' message of love with others.

This book is for you.

During 2020, in the midst of the COVID shutdown and the national election, Rev. Dr. Stan Copeland wrote this social media post:

> I worship at a place called "Lovers Lane". Yes, we are United Methodist but more importantly we aspire to be "lovers" of God and one another. We live in a politically charged world that does not value "united", rather the "us" and "them" approach to life seems to rule the day. Still we Christian-types follow a man named Jesus who taught a brand of love that took the ten commandments to a higher

standard. Let's not forget that he said, "You have heard it said of old, 'Thou shalt not murder', but if you have hate in your heart you have already killed someone." He continues, "If someone strikes you on the cheek, present the other side of your face for a swing. Retaliate with my brand of love." Then Jesus said, "Love your enemies and pray for those who persecute or hate you." Nobody is begging for these sayings to be posted on a public wall, but we followers of Jesus, aspire to live this odd, others-oriented way. And when we live out these guiding principles and somebody wonders what is wrong with us, we can blame it on Jesus.

Stan is the senior pastor of Lovers Lane United Methodist Church in Dallas, Texas, where I serve as an associate pastor and my husband Jeff works as an executive director. As you will read later in the book, Stan has been an instrumental person in my life of ministry. I'm always inspired by his writing and his preaching, so it's no surprise that this post would stick in my head.

I remember reading it and thinking, "Blame it on Jesus. Now that would make a great song!"

Fast forward to 2023. I'm sitting with my songwriting partners, Randy Austin and Rafe Grigar, and I pitch the idea for a song based on Stan's words, "Blame it on Jesus." The doubt was written all over their confused faces.

I envisioned this song reclaiming Jesus' message of love from all the people who use Jesus to justify prejudice and hate. Those voices are just too loud. It's time to start using Jesus' words to fight back with love.

It was as if a light bulb turned on over their heads. At Lovers Lane, I serve as the pastor of the Crosswalk worship community, and together the three of us lead worship with our band, Lovers Lane Worship. Every Sunday, I preach about Jesus' love and acceptance for ALL people, and we sing songs that reinforce that message. God continues to bring the misfits of the world to our doors where they truly experience a community of love and grace.

When we finished writing the song, Randy said to me, "DeDe this is your coming out song." And in many ways he is right. As you will read in the chapters ahead, much of my life experience has led me to this moment. I spent the early part of my career in Christian music, where you have to follow certain rules to be successful. As I moved into church ministry, I have faced rejection and spent time in my own wilderness discovering who I really am. But I've also met many people along the way who have influenced and inspired me. Some of their stories are in this book as well.

Now, at Lovers Lane UMC since 2014, I'm at a church whose mission statement is "Loving ALL people into relationship with Jesus Christ" and I have discovered the freedom described in the chorus of this song we wrote, "Blame It":

Hate won't break me, or tear me apart
I'm fighting back with love, aimin' straight for the heart
I'm shakin' things up!
If you don't like the reasons,
Take it to the cross and
Blame it on Jesus!

When Jeff heard "Blame It" for the first time, he said "I think there's a book in that song." Keep in mind that neither of us has ever written a book. But Jeff knows my story and we share a commitment to helping people accept God's love in Christ and then to share God's love in Christ with others.

I love to preach. Jeff loves to put words on paper. So, we thought we'd make a good team for this book. We've enjoyed reminiscing about where God has brought us and looking forward to where God is taking us. We hope you enjoy it too.

What's Ahead

For us to stand up for the misfits in our lives—the marginalized, the forgotten, the rejected—we need to understand Jesus' true message of love and acceptance. How else can we counter other messages that use scripture to hold people back and push people down?

We have taken the lyrics of "Blame It" to identify seven key lessons we can learn from Jesus:

1. **The Power of Words.** From comforting the brokenhearted to challenging oppressive systems, Jesus' language teaches us how to speak with purpose and compassion.

2. **Embrace the Misfits.** Jesus gives us a few steps to understanding, relating to and finding compassion for others—even when we don't understand them.

3. **Face the Critics.** Jesus shows us that love, grace, and mercy are far more important than worrying about what others think.

4. **Pick Your Battles.** Jesus knows his mission on earth is to fulfill God's plan, not to get bogged down by every dispute or challenge others bring his way.

5. **Use Love as a Weapon.** Jesus' love is not an emotion, but an action that seeks the ultimate good of others.

6. **Shake Things Up.** When Jesus is challenged, he engages deeply with the people in it, even those who are morally questionable by the standards of the day.

7. **Take it to the Cross.** Turning our burdens, sins, struggles, or challenges over to Jesus gives us the confidence and strength to be the voice of love in a world of hate.

Because in many ways this is my story about what I've learned from Jesus, and to prevent any confusion, we've written this book in my voice. If a person is listed without a last name, their name has been changed. All other people with first and last names are real and important people in our lives. All scripture, unless specifically noted, is quoted from the Common English Bible.

We hope that when you've finished this book, you will be ready to stand up for the misfits in your life and when people ask you what in the world you're doing, you will have the confidence to respond, "Blame it on Jesus!"

Chapter 1
THE POWER OF WORDS

"**W**ELL, YOUR MINISTRY HERE has obviously been a mistake."

Those were the words spoken to me by Luci, the newly installed pastor of the church where I was serving as the music director. It was our first one-on-one meeting, and it was supposed to be an opportunity for us to get to know each other: she, the new pastor, and I, the long-time staff member.

I had high hopes for this relationship. Luci was the first female pastor I had worked for. I assumed she understood the unique challenges of serving in church ministry as someone who wasn't an old white man.

The church was a mid-sized congregation in a suburb of Fort Worth, Texas. I'd been on staff as the Music Director for almost nine years, and Luci was the fourth pastor I would work under there. We were a small staff, so my duties stretched beyond the typical responsibilities of a music director. Over the years, I built deep relationships with the people of this church. I visited them in the hospital when they had babies, and I visited them in the hospital when they were ill. I walked with them through the joy of weddings, and I walked with them through the despair of divorce. I was there for their everyday concerns, challenges, and joys.

None of these roles was a burden to me. I saw them as part of my call to ministry. I knew God had placed me in those moments to help shine his light during people's best and worst times. I was honored to serve in that way.

When I met with Pastor Luci that day, I shared these thoughts with her. Sitting across from her, I described my time at this church, expressing gratitude for the opportunities I'd had to serve and my eagerness to partner with her in the future.

As I finished, she looked at me and with a dismissive flutter of her eyes, said, "Well, your ministry here has obviously been a mistake." She went on to explain that, as I was only the music director and not an ordained pastor, these responsibilities were never meant to be mine. She assured me that I would no longer be needed in those capacities.

At least that's what I think she went on to explain. Honestly, at that moment, I flashed back to the night I learned about the death of Melanie Goodwin, a young woman who had been on my praise team and was now a freshman in a college not too far from home.

I was on my way home from seeing a touring production of "The Lion King" with two friends. Melanie had been the one who told me, "You just have to see this show!" She loved everything musical and theater.

When I left the theater, I had a message from Glen, Melanie's father, asking me to contact him as soon as possible. I called him from the car on my way home, and he asked me to pull over because he had some difficult news.

I'll never forget Glen telling me that the remains of Melanie's body had been found in her burned-out car, hidden behind an office building in a nearby city. At that moment, the details that led to that horror weren't yet clear. But over the next day, we would learn that Melanie had been kidnapped, raped, and murdered after stopping at a convenience store on her way from her job back to her dorm. I don't remember much of the rest of my drive home. But I do remember Jeff waiting for me on the front step of our house and me crying in his arms as we stood in the yard.

Our pastor at the time was on medical leave, so it was my responsibility to support the Goodwin family. The Goodwins were a large, loving clan with a big presence in our church. From the moment I'd joined this church staff, the Goodwins had welcomed me and made me feel like a part of their own family. "Unc" and "Auntie" had become the names I called Melanie's parents. Supporting this family during this difficult time was much more than a responsibility that fell to me by default. It was where God had prepared me to be at this moment.

Melanie was beautiful inside and out. Her big personality lit up every room she entered. We'd become friends as she grew up singing on my praise team. She had a beautiful voice. Jeff and I saw her play the "Fairy Godmother" in a local production of "Cinderella" shortly before she left for college. She stole the show! She was kind-hearted. To know Melanie was to love her.

Just a few days before her death, Jeff and I took our newborn son Owen to see her lead worship at her college Wesley Foundation. One of my favorite memories of Melanie is watching her hold Owen that day, cooing and doting over him as if he were her own brother or nephew.

It was a devastating time. The Goodwins, our church family, her high school friends, her theater community, her new college family, my family, me—we were all shattered. I did my best to support the Goodwins through their grief and the trial that eventually put the killer in jail two years later. Many long days and even longer nights were spent with the family and friends, followed by tearful evenings at home with my husband. I was proud of how the Goodwins and our church faced this tragedy and honored to stand by them as their de facto pastor.

I still remember this time as one of the most pivotal moments in my ministry. The experience has informed so much of what I know and do as a pastor today.

So when Pastor Luci told me my ministry was a mistake, I was stunned. I couldn't imagine how this could be true, but my shock left me silent. Luci finished the conversation by thanking me for "filling in the gaps," but she made it clear she would handle things from here on out. I left her office angry and hurt.

Even as a child, I knew the phrase "sticks and stones may break my bones, but words will never hurt me" was more wishful thinking than truth. We often recited it as a defense when someone said something hurtful. But as I grew older, I learned that the wounds from sticks and stones healed far faster than those inflicted by words spoken in hate, hurt, or malice.

Words matter. What we say to one another matters.

In hindsight, maybe I shouldn't have let Luci's words affect me so deeply. The fact remains that I was hurt by someone I thought I could trust and with whom I could build a relationship. It was the beginning of the end of my time at that church, but, as is so often the case when we allow God to lead, it was also the beginning of something much more.

Words Matter

I don't want to sound like your Memaw, but I'm concerned about the growing lack of respect for others in how we use our words. In the good ol' days (the opening phrase of any Memaw's critique), people were kinder to one another. Now, we are more comfortable using language that tears others down when we disagree rather than engaging in respectful conversations about our differences.

The way we talk matters. The words we choose matter. How we treat one another matters.

We have two opportunities when we use our tongues to speak: to use them as weapons to hurt or to use them as tools for healing. The things that give our lives meaning—music, movies, books, poetry—are all born from words. But just as words can uplift, they can also destroy.

Too often, we Christians get caught up in the rules of how we're supposed to live, holding our Bibles in one hand and wagging our fingers with the other. Even when the injustices we highlight are valid, if our words cause others to disengage from the conversation, we've lost the opportunity to make a difference.

The point of our faith is love. It's not about casting out demons—that's Jesus' job. Let's be real: when we put the rules before true understanding, we push people away instead of pulling them close. People often need a listening ear more than a lecture on what's right. If we're not listening we will miss someone's cry for help or their need for a bit of grace.

THE POINT OF OUR FAITH IS LOVE. IT'S NOT ABOUT CASTING OUT DEMONS—THAT'S JESUS' JOB.

Think about it—true healing starts with seeing and hearing people, not just sizing them up based on rules. Healing begins by connecting heart to heart, showing that you care more about them than the guidelines. Healing can begin when people feel heard and understood, not just as rule followers but as individuals with real struggles and stories.

James the Just

James, the brother of Jesus, has often been called "James the Just" because of his unwavering commitment to righteousness and fair treatment for all. Putting people first resonates powerfully with his teachings. In his New Testament letter, James emphasizes the importance of practicing one's faith in practical, caring ways. He's the one who famously said, "Faith without works is dead." Our faith isn't based on following religious rules alone, but also on how those beliefs translate into acts of kindness and fairness towards others. This includes the words we choose.

James' focus on justice and practical Christianity reminds us to prioritize people over simple adherence to rules. Our actions, the words we choose, and how we treat others are the truest expressions of our faith. Putting other people first leads us to live out the justice that James advocated, showing the world a true faith that acts, loves, and serves.

Small but Powerful

James emphasizes the importance of the words we choose in this effort. He says, "Even though the tongue is a small part of the body, it boasts wildly. Think about this: A small flame can set a whole forest on fire. The tongue is a small flame of fire, a world of evil at work in us. It contaminates our entire lives. Because of it, the circle of life is set on fire. The tongue itself is set on fire by the flames of hell" (James 3:5-6).

Wow! Those are some strong words. As small it is, the tongue has the ability to burn it all down. Have you ever met someone with a really sharp tongue? You say one wrong word to them, and it's like a second personality comes out and they cut you to shreds with their words. The scary thing about words is that once they've been said, there's no taking them back.

Even our fists can't cause as much pain as our words. One punch can cause immediate physical damage to a person, but one wag of the tongue can cause wounds that never heal. Unlike physical injuries, the injury inflicted by words can leave deep and lasting scars.

Far Reach

The tongue carries immense reach as the instrument we use to express our thoughts, beliefs, and emotions. A single word can resonate far beyond its initial utterance, influencing minds, shaping opinions, and even altering the course of events. Think about how a hurtful comment, carelessly posted online, can spread like wildfire, affecting not just the individual to whom it was directed, but also rippling through entire communities. In seconds, words can spread around the globe, touching the lives of people we've never met.

During the 2024 Paris Olympics, Algerian boxer Imane Khelif faced Italian boxer Angela Carini in an opening bout of the women's welterweight boxing tournament. Forty-six seconds into the match, after receiving a few punches, Carini ended the fight early because of severe nose pain from one of Khelif's blows.

As Khelif began to celebrate her unusual win, social media lit up with reports that she was a transgender woman. Only, it wasn't true. Khelif is an Algerian boxer who has always identified as a woman and has been competing as a woman at the international level for years. She has even described how as a young girl she excelled at football in her rural village home. The boys often felt threatened and picked fights with her. Her ability to dodge the boys' punches led her to boxing.

What should have been a day of celebration for her became something completely different. With little or no thought to the outcome, people used vile, hurtful language to spread falsehoods about a person who they knew nothing about.

Violence of Words

In another time, the Pharisees bring a woman accused of adultery before Jesus. A crowd gathers, eager to stone her to death—the required punishment of the day for adultery. In an effort to show him up, the Pharisees try to get Jesus to agree to condemn this woman to death. But in a twist that only Jesus could create, his words turn the situation upside down. He says to the crowd, "Whoever is without sin, cast the first stone." Slowly, the mob realizes that to throw the stone would reveal their own hypocrisy.

I've never understood the idea of stoning another person. The violence of it boggles my mind. How do ordinary people, neighbors, shopkeepers, friends become angry enough to pick up stones and throw them at a woman?

How do people on the other side of the world spread life-changing, pain-causing misinformation about a woman boxer they don't even know?

The only explanation is hate. Hate of a woman. Hate of something they don't understand. Hate of their personal situations. Hate that begins with accusations. Hate that begins with self-righteous indignation. Hate that starts with words.

The Origin of Hate

This abuse of language starts at the top. When our leaders—whether in government, corporations, families, or churches—choose words that minimize or denigrate people because they look different, think differently, vote differently, it has real consequences for our communities. It normalizes and emboldens the rest of us to use the same kind of language.

We look to our leaders for cues on how to behave, especially in situations of conflict or disagreement. Their divisive language normalizes and empowers the rest of us to use the same kind of language. We become comfortable expressing our frustrations, disagreements, or beliefs in more confrontational and aggressive ways.

As the threshold for civil discourse has lowered, what might have once been considered extreme or unacceptable has become part of everyday conversation. This kind of talk leads to a breakdown of how we live in community, as we become more dug-in to the extreme side of our views and less willing to engage in constructive dialogue. This language of division drives a wedge between groups and individuals, leading to more division and conflict.

The Antidote to Hate

As Christians, Jesus calls us to a higher standard. Jesus calls us to love God *and* to love one another. Love is the bottom line. Love wins over everything else.

Here's the simple truth: hate divides and love connects. Where hate builds walls, love opens doors and windows, letting fresh perspectives and new light flood in. Love teaches us empathy, urging us to step into another's shoes, feel their joys and pains, and understand their journey.

When we choose love, we see beyond differences and focus on the things that bind us. Love compels us to listen, really listen, to others' stories, which often reveal that the roots of their fears and prejudices aren't so different from our own.

> WHERE HATE BUILDS WALLS, LOVE OPENS DOORS AND WINDOWS, LETTING FRESH PERSPECTIVES AND NEW LIGHT FLOOD IN.

And words of love don't just sit back. They act. They lead us to reach across the table to help, to heal, to unite. It's the hand extended in forgiveness, the embrace after a long feud, the kind word in a tense room. By actively loving, we disrupt the cycle of hate and create new patterns of mutual respect and acceptance.

The irony is that choosing not to speak at all can be just as harmful as speaking with hate. I've struggled with this in my own life, often failing to use my voice when it could have brought healing. It's a moral failure I continue to work on. We are responsible for speaking up for those who can't speak for themselves. That's what Jesus did.

In a world often overshadowed by division, choosing words of love is a powerful stance against hate. It's not always easy, but it's always worth it because love is the most effective tool we have to create a community where everyone feels valued and included.

The only antidote to hate is love.

Just as words can cause great harm in hate, they can also heal in love.

Encouragement, praise, and truth spoken in love can lift spirits, inspire change, and build connections. When we choose our words wisely, we can bring light into darkness, hope into despair, and peace into conflict.

Words of Transformation

Jesus' words throughout his ministry show us how we can use our own words as instruments of change. From comforting the brokenhearted to challenging oppressive systems, Jesus uses his voice to bring transformation. His language teaches us how to speak with purpose and compassion.

Healing Words. A man with leprosy approaches Jesus, saying, "Lord, if you are willing, you can make me clean." Jesus simply replies, "I am willing. Be clean!" With those simple words, the man is healed immediately (Matthew 8:2-3). Jesus' words bring physical and emotional healing to a man cast out from society.

Hopeful Words. In his Sermon on the Mount, Jesus begins with the Beatitudes, which offer hope to the poor in spirit, those who mourn, and the meek (Matthew 5-7). He reverses the expectations of the time by promising that the kingdom of heaven belongs to them, not the powerful or the privileged. His words give hope to the overlooked and left-out, saying that God's favor rested on them and that a better future is possible.

Restful Words. Jesus later says, "Come to me, all you who are struggling hard and carrying heavy loads, and I will give you rest" (Matthew 11:28). His words offer profound hope to those struggling with the weight of life's challenges. In a world that can be harsh and demanding, Jesus promises rest, relief, and renewal to all who come to him. His words invite us to find solace in God's love, especially in difficult times.

Restoring Words. Jesus' words are always rooted in love. His command to "love your neighbor as yourself" (Matthew 22:39) encapsulates the heart of his ministry. Jesus extends love to everyone, including those who betray him. After denying Jesus three times, Peter is transformed by Jesus' words, "Feed my sheep," which restore him and call him to lead the early church.

Forgiving Words. On the cross, in the midst of his own suffering, He prays for those who are crucifying him, saying, "Father, forgive them, for they do not know what they are doing" (Luke 23:34). Even in his darkest moment, Jesus' words are filled with love and mercy, offering forgiveness to those who had wronged him.

Words matter. When we follow the example of Jesus, our words can also heal broken hearts, offer hope to those who are struggling, and spread love and forgiveness to everyone we encounter. The power of words is immense, and by speaking as Jesus did, we can bring transformation and light into the world.

When Randy, Rafe and I wrote and recorded the song "Blame It," we tried to follow the example of Jesus with a message of healing, hope, and love. The words of the song advocate for inclusivity and support of people who often feel marginalized and overlooked. We hope it inspires a sense of solidarity and community among listeners who relate to feeling different or not fitting into mainstream expectations.

An early line in the song says, "People started talkin', when I broke down some doors for the misfits put in my life." After we released the song, I'll never forget the first time I saw someone post "#teammisfit" on social media.

The teammisfit hashtag has become a banner under which people can rally. It gives them a way to express their connection to the song's message, share their own experiences, and participate in a larger conversation about acceptance and diversity. We even printed "#teammisfit" hats and t-shirts!

When used in love, a word like "misfit" gets redefined as a word of inclusion and hope. After all, we are all misfits in one way or another. When we accept that about ourselves, we can begin to have more compassion and love for people who aren't just like us.

When we listen to others before responding, we begin to understand different perspectives and see ourselves in them. We will never grow if we live alone in our own little bubbles.

When we listen to the thoughts and ideas of people who aren't just like us, our bubble begins to grow bigger. When we fill our lives with people who think, look, and act just like us, we never learn anything new. When we invite the misfits in as our own brothers and sisters, our perspectives grow, and our ability to love becomes endless.

As we welcome more people into our community who aren't just like us, we also become increasingly aware of the consequences of our words. As we hear the stories of others who were hurt by the reckless words of thoughtless people, we recognize even more the power we have to either edify or destroy.

I am ashamed of the words I might have spoken in my past that caused someone else hurt or pain. I ask forgiveness of those people. I ask forgiveness from God. And now I ask that God fill my heart and my tongue with words that will heal.

Every word we speak or type is like a seed. It can grow into something beautiful and life-giving or something destructive and damaging. As stewards of this powerful tool, we must be deliberate in how we use it, understanding that with great power comes great responsibility. Our words are not just fleeting sounds or letters on a screen. They are the building blocks of relationships, reputations, and realities.

We can begin by speaking truthfully, kindly, and constructively, always seeking to reflect Christ in our words.

A few years ago, I found myself in another pastor's office at the final interview for another music ministry job. It had been three years since I'd left my position with Pastor Luci, and I'd followed a bumpy path through a couple of short-lived stints at other churches. This was going to be my last stop. I had reached the point where I wondered if God was trying to tell me to serve in another way.

This time, I sat across from a man named Stan Copeland in his large office at Lovers Lane United Methodist Church. Stan, just shy of 60 years old with an impossibly thick shock of dark brown hair, greeted me warmly. When he spoke, I noticed the remnants of his East Texas accent.

One of the first things I remember telling him was that I wasn't sure I was really meant for church ministry. This was a job interview, and as I look back, I wonder what I was thinking. But I felt an immediate trust and kinship with this man who I'd only met in passing one other time at a church conference.

In response to my declaration of doubt, he said without a pause, "In fact, I know that you are qualified beyond the job we have in mind for you. I know that you have gifts you don't even know about that God has called you to use."

I'll never forget those words.

We talked for an hour about everything but the job. We discussed our faith, our families, and times we both had been at death's door. For a moment, we both had tears in our eyes.

Stan's words were a healing moment for me.

Five years later, I walked into his office again, tentatively telling him that I thought God was calling me to ordained ministry. I expected him to encourage me cautiously, maybe give me a book to read, and tell me to pray on it.

What he said was, "Well, what have you been waiting for?"

Words matter.

The Weight of Words

In *The Road Less Traveled*, M. Scott Peck discusses the importance of authentic communication and taking responsibility for our words: "The truth is that our finest moments are most likely to occur when we are feeling deeply uncomfortable, unhappy, or unfulfilled. For it is only in such moments, propelled by our discomfort, that we are likely to step out of our ruts and start searching for different ways or truer answers."

We all know the dual nature of the tongue because we've all used our own to tear down and to lift up. Our voices are intertwined with memories of shame and moments of hope.

We must figure out how to live together with different opinions. We may not always agree, but we can disagree with grace. Living in a world where we all think the same would be boring—there would be no growth, no opportunity to learn or to change.

Jesus calls us to love God first and to love one another as we would love ourselves. We can't truly love one another if we don't even know one another.

To battle hate—to stand up against it—our voices must reflect what we stand for more than what we stand against. Standing against something leads to hate; standing for something starts with love. Let's stand for each other!

Every word we speak carries weight. Whether we choose to lift others up or tear them down, the impact is profound. Let's choose our words with the care and love that Jesus taught us. Then when someone questions our words spoken in love, we can say, "Blame it on Jesus."

Of course, the implication here is that we are going to use our words to not just uplift the people like us, but also the outcast, the marginalized, the misfits. In the next chapter, we will begin the hard work of embracing the misfits, the people the world wants to discard. Until we know and understand the things we fear, we can't truly stand up for them in love.

Chapter 2
EMBRACE THE MISFITS

FOR MUCH OF MY life I made my living as a singer. The first time I sang in public, I was 2 ½ years old. My mom set me up on a stool at the Grapevine Opry in Grapevine, Texas, and I sang "This Little Light of Mine". By the time I was 10 years old, I was traveling with my mom's gospel quartet singing with her at events all over Texas, Louisiana, Arkansas, and Mississippi. Sometimes, it felt like I led a double-life. I went to school all week and hopped on a bus to go who-knows-where every weekend.

When I turned 21, I got a contract to sing on the world's largest Christian television network. For about 10 years, I divided my time between my job on TV and traveling from church to church singing in worship and concerts. It was an eye-opening experience. I met some of the most well-known evangelists the world had ever seen. The stories I could tell. But I won't.

Throughout that time, I had mixed feelings about my television career. Many of the people I met had truly authentic relationships with God and, as far as I could tell, pure motives in their ministries. Even if I wasn't always in sync with their theology, I found them to be kind, loving people who genuinely wanted the world to know God.

Then there were the others. People with whom my experience was not as positive. Their message focused more on the damnation of God's word than God's love. With them, I often had the feeling that with one wrong step I would be cast from God's good graces. And even if I weren't cast from God's good graces, I would certainly be cast from theirs.

The list of "thou shalt nots" was long: drinking, smoking, gambling, sex (all kinds of "shalt nots" about sex), divorce, fashion, and more. They were quick to pass judgment when someone else had a "moral failure". They also knew that their "friends" in faith would be quick to pass judgment on them should they succumb to their own temptations. That often led to a spirit of personal secrets and disingenuous lives.

I understood the need to keep your life private. I was living in an unhappy marriage at the time. At least it was unhappy on my side of it. On the other side, there was abuse and infidelity. I was miserable. But I was afraid to tell anyone because I thought that to divorce my husband would be the end of my career. I worked in a world where divorce—especially by the wife—was not tolerated. I feared becoming an outcast in the world I had created for myself.

But the time came where I couldn't stay in my marriage any longer. I divorced my husband.

It wasn't something I could keep a secret. I approached the woman who led the network and told her what I was doing. I explained to her that for my own safety, sanity, and self-respect, I could no longer stay in my marriage.

I fully expected her to tell me that my time with the network had come to an end. Or at the very least, I would have to take a break until the stain of my divorce had faded.

But that's not what happened.

She pulled me aside, sat me down, and looked at me with concern in her eyes. With my hands in hers, she assured me that I still had a home there, and if anyone tried to tell me otherwise, I should send them to her.

At that moment, when I had lost one home, I was welcomed into another. It was the first time I understood what it felt like to be looked upon as an outcast—a misfit—but to be made welcome in a place I didn't expect to be.

It's not a feeling I forgot.

Embracing the Misfits

It's not always easy to connect with people who are different from us. It's a whole lot easier to surround ourselves with people just like us. Jesus gives us a few clues to understanding, relating to, and finding compassion for others—even when we don't understand them.

Look at our own lives first. It starts with recognizing our own short-comings. Jesus says, "Why do you see the splinter that's in your brother's or sister's eye, but don't notice the log in your own eye?" (Matthew 7:3). Why are we trying to fix other people's sins or hold other people's issues against them? We've got our own baggage to carry, empty, and clean out.

This could be one of the biggest challenges for most of us every-day Christians. We can be really good at pointing out the faults of our brothers and sisters. Then we get all high and mighty when someone wants to call out our flaws.

Consider the fruit, not just what you think you see. Jesus warns us about "false prophets" who appear righteous on the outside, but inwardly are "ravenous wolves." He says, "...by their fruit you will recognize them" (Matthew 7:15-20). In other words, we can't really know someone by what we see because we reveal our true character in how we live, especially in how we treat other people.

You might say to me, "I don't think it's appropriate for a pastor to have purple hair. They won't take you seriously." Well, bless your heart! What you don't know is that the color of my hair has opened more doors to have conversations with people I would have never met.

I don't know why, but people feel comfortable talking to me about my purple hair. At the grocery store, the post office, department stores, walking down the street. I even had someone yell out the car window as they drove past me in a shopping center.

Every time (well not when they drive by), I am able to respond with a heartfelt thank you and a kind word to them as well. "You would look great with purple hair too." Or "You look beautiful in that color you're wearing."

We all want to be seen. When someone says something kind to me and I respond with a kind word to them, we create a connection. It opens the door for me to ask about their day, or the children they have with them, or what else they have planned for their day.

We all need to be seen. If my purple hair gives me an opportunity to be a loving pastor to another person—even for the briefest moment—I welcome it.

So, you don't judge my purple hair and I won't judge your Crocs. Really, I think Crocs would have been one of the "thou shalt not" list of items to wear if they'd existed in biblical times. But you do you.

Approach everyone with compassion, not judgment. Jesus condemns the Pharisees for the self-righteous, hypocritical attitudes they have when they point out the sins of others. Jesus ain't playing here. He says, "For they tie together heavy packs that are impossible to carry. They put them on the shoulders of others, but are unwilling to lift a finger to move them" (Matthew 23:4).

Sin is a real thing. It's not something we should ignore. Iron sharpens iron. Part of being a community of faith is to learn from one another. It's to hold one another accountable. So, there is a role in identifying our sins to one another.

But the misfits in our world are often defined by strangers' perception of their sin. What they do wrong. The choices they make. Who they claim to be. So to think that someone should be cast out or hated because of how we define sin is short-sighted at best, ignorant in the least, and hateful at the worst.

If our goal as people of faith is to identify the sins of others so we can cast them out of the club, then we've missed the point. We're all sinners. That's a fact. Like it or not. We will never be able to truly welcome all people, if we hold ourselves up as more righteous than even one other person. Accepting our shortcomings and taking off our masks can be freeing. Acknowledging that we are all sinners gives us one more point of connection with each other and makes our witness more authentic.

Growing up, my house was filled with all kinds of people. I come from a musical family and have an eclectic extended family—blood family and chosen family. My parents never turned anyone away from our door. To everyone my dad was, "Daddy Large" and my mom was "Mama Merle." Weekends were filled with people from all walks of life. Dad loved to cook big meals and to make everyone feel welcome. Someone was always playing at the piano with people gathered around singing.

I knew many of the people in our home were different. But as a young girl, I didn't understand how. There was one man, Wilson, who stands out in my memory. I loved Wilson. He was close in age to my parents.

When he was in our house, he was full of life. He had the most vibrant personality. He had the best time singing, and he told the funniest stories. He was always laughing and treated me so kindly. He brought me presents. Beautiful dresses and little purses and shoes.

This was before "Don't Ask, Don't Tell" was an official policy of the U.S. military. Don't ask, don't tell was just a way of life for gay people at that time (LGBTQ+ wasn't a thing yet either). If you didn't ask a person if they were gay and they didn't tell you they were gay, you could both just go on being friends pretending they weren't gay. At least that was the thought.

The unwritten policy put straight people at ease and helped gay people feel safe. But to a young girl, it created confusion.

It was a few years later that I began to understand that Wilson was a gay man. Late one night, my parents left the house in a hurry. It wasn't until the next day that I found out they'd been called to bail Wilson out of jail. No one ever told me why, but I heard the gossip and I could see that Wilson was too ashamed to ever talk about it.

Even in a time when being gay was still not accepted, it didn't matter to me. I knew Wilson. I loved Wilson. He was a kind, funny, and talented man. I didn't need to know anything else.

I didn't really know until I was an adult how lucky I was to grow up in a home where ALL people were welcomed and loved. My parents were people of deep faith, and they wanted to love the way Jesus did. I thought that was how all people of faith would be.

Mom and Dad taught me what it meant to offer a safe place for the misfits in life. They knew that in some way, we are all misfits, and that life is so much richer when the people around us who don't look, act, think, or live exactly like us. We are smarter, stronger, and more empathetic when we live that way.

Jesus' Misfits

When we think about Jesus and the people he chooses to follow him, we see how different his disciples were from each other. Jesus doesn't pick people who are the same. He purposefully chooses a group with different backgrounds, personalities, and even beliefs. Jesus' knows that diversity makes life richer.

Jesus chooses fishermen, a tax collector, and even a zealot—people who probably would not hang out together otherwise. Think about it. Simon Peter is a passionate, impulsive fisherman, while Matthew is a tax collector, who is most likely considered a traitor by his fellow Jews. Then there's Simon the Zealot, who is deeply political and probably has strong feelings about someone like Matthew working for the Romans. But Jesus brings them all together, knowing that their individual differences will actually make them stronger as a group.

When we surround ourselves with people who think differently and who have had different life experiences, we open ourselves up to new ways of seeing the world. These different perspectives don't just help us understand more—they challenge us to grow, to be better, and to see beyond ourselves.

In the church, we talk about being the body of Christ, where every part has a unique role to play. Just like the hand can't do what the eye does, and the ear can't replace the foot, each of us has something unique to offer. When we embrace diversity—whether it's cultural, ideological, or just personal experiences—we create a more vibrant and healthy community. We start to see that our way isn't the only way, and that other people's insights can help us grow closer to God and to each other.

WHEN WE SURROUND OURSELVES WITH PEOPLE WHO THINK DIFFERENTLY AND WHO HAVE HAD DIFFERENT LIFE EXPERIENCES, WE OPEN OURSELVES UP TO NEW WAYS OF SEEING THE WORLD.

Growing Through Challenges

In many ways it would be easier to associate only with people who look like us, who think the way we do, and who see the world through a similar lens. It would be boring, but it would be easier.

Jesus shows us that real growth comes when we're challenged. His disciples don't always see eye-to-eye, and there are plenty of times when they disagree with each other—and even with Jesus. But these moments of tension lead to growth. They learn how to love each other despite

their differences, to forgive one another, and to work together toward a common goal.

In our own lives, when we choose to associate with people who challenge us, we're stepping out of our comfort zones. And let's be honest—that's not always easy. But it's in those uncomfortable places that we grow the most. These relationships teach us to be humble, patient, and gracious. They remind us that we don't have all the answers, and that God often speaks to us through others—especially those who aren't like us.

Jesus' disciples also show us what the kingdom of God looks like. In the book of Revelation, we get a picture of heaven where people from every nation, tribe, and language gather together, worshiping God. This isn't just a future reality—it's something Jesus calls us to work toward today.

We're showing that the love of Christ is bigger than any human division and that his grace is enough for everyone. Building this kind of inclusive community doesn't happen by accident. It takes intentionality and a willingness to be uncomfortable. But this is what Jesus asks of us, and the reward is a deeper, richer faith.

When we embrace our differences, it's not just to make life more interesting—it's following Jesus' call to love and include everyone. We become more compassionate, more understanding, and more like Christ. We start to see the image of God in people who are different from us, and in doing so, we share the love of Christ with people who need it.

Choosing Ignorance

Recently, riots broke out in England over a social media post that an illegal immigrant had stabbed and killed a mother and her child. But even when the post was proven to be untrue, the riots continued. People continued to stir the turmoil because *"it could have been true."*

WHEN WE EMBRACE OUR DIFFERENCES, IT'S NOT JUST TO MAKE LIFE MORE INTERESTING—IT'S FOLLOWING JESUS' CALL TO LOVE AND INCLUDE EVERYONE.

We would rather live in ignorance than to educate ourselves about the facts.

In some ways life seems to be improving for some people who have been historically outcast. Women have gained greater access to education, healthcare, and leadership roles, while laws supporting gender equality and protections against harassment have been strengthened. LGBTQ+ rights have advanced through the legalization of same-sex marriage, anti-discrimination laws, and greater social acceptance. Immigrants have benefited from more inclusive immigration policies, legal protections, and movements advocating for refugee rights and humane treatment.

But even then, there seems to be a tenuousness to it, as if all of these advances could be turned back at any moment. Just as some gain more access to their basic rights, it's as if others in the church become more emboldened to oppose them.

While many denominations recognize women's call to ordained ministry, others dig in deeper to deny them. As the LGBTQ+ community begins to gain more rights, religious leaders campaign to revoke their newly acquired legal protections, and denominations split over theological differences around homosexuality. As many communities welcome legal immigrants as essential to their economies, others fight harder and harder to reject and mistreat people based on race and nationality.

We come to judgment more quickly than ever before—on both ends of the spectrum. People hold their beliefs so strongly that we are unwilling to listen to differing thoughts. We'd rather live in ignorance than educate ourselves of the facts.

Finding Common Ground

Churches are filled with people who call out other people who don't live the way they think they should. We often use our Bibles to virtually beat other people over the head. When we stop swinging our Bibles and start getting to know one another first, we might discover that we have a lot of common ground.

It's the common ground we have lost. We become so adamant about our own stand on a position that we ignore what we share. We're all human beings trying to survive in a difficult world. We work to pay the bills. We have children that we cherish one minute and are vexed by the next. We create lives with husband and wives. We get stuck in traffic. We enjoy great meals. We suffer from illness. We celebrate birthdays. The list is endless.

We can rarely see another person's whole story. That's the advantage that God has. God knows us from the inside out. So, when someone's different or out of the box or we don't understand, God does.

Several years ago, a friend of mine started a church called Citichurch. He asked me if I would help lead the music. Honestly, it wasn't long after my experience with Pastor Luci and I wasn't sure I was ready to step back into church work. But I committed to helping him for a couple of months.

The church met in a small store front near the Dallas neighborhood where I grew up. On the first Sunday night, I arrived not long before the service began. As I drove into the parking lot, an old yellow school bus pulled up near me. A large group of what appeared to be homeless people got off the bus and entered the front doors of the church. There were men and women. They represented every possible skin color. Some were old. Some were young. They were all adults. Their clothes were well-used and their shoes were worn. They walked slowly with the weight of life on their backs.

As I entered the church behind them, scattered throughout the room were other people who had arrived before the bus. Well dressed and actively preparing for worship, they were noticeably different from the busload of people. Many of them stood at the door with smiles to welcome the people who had arrived on the bus. Others remained seated as they waited for worship to begin.

A young man greeted me warmly. After introducing me to his partner, another young man, I told him I was there to help lead worship. He led me to the room where the pastor and the worship team were meeting.

Throughout the evening, as I met more and more people, I realized the congregation was fairly evenly divided between people from the homeless shelter and people from the LGBTQ+ community. There were a few of us straight folk there too, but we were in the minority.

It had been a long time since I really felt the Holy Spirit moving as I did in worship that night. It reminded me of being back in my parents' home. First, the music was phenomenal. But even more importantly, I was in a place where everyone was welcome. No questions asked.

This wasn't a "gay" church. These people hadn't come together because of their sexuality. They came together because they love God. They welcomed this group of homeless people into their church because they knew what it was like to be cast out and made to feel unwelcome by church people. They found common ground.

My understanding of "Don't Ask, Don't Tell" got redefined during my time at this small church in a store front in West Dallas. Here, I met people who lived their lives unapologetically the way God created them. They knew it. I knew it. They didn't need to tell it. I didn't need to ask it. It didn't matter, because we both knew that we all were children of God.

A Question of Homosexuality

You might be uncomfortable with the idea that the Holy Spirit would be present in a church full of LGBTQ+ people. How could that be possible if homosexuality is a sin? Let's talk about two possible ways to address that question:

1. **Homosexuality is a sin.** Let's say you've read the Bible and you understand it to say that homosexuality is a sin. Or let's say you've heard a pastor or a teacher explain to you why the Bible says homosexuality is a sin.

   So what.

   I'm really tired of people cherry-picking sins from the Bible that they want to punish and hold people accountable for. When the Pharisee asked Jesus, "What is the most important law in the Bible?", Jesus didn't say, "You know, that one about being gay."

   Jesus answered:

   "You must love the Lord your God with all your heart, with all your being, and with all your mind. This is the first and greatest commandment. And the second is like it: You must love your neighbor as you love yourself" (Matthew 22:37-39).

   Period.

In fact, Jesus never says anything about homosexuality. Whether we understand homosexuality to be a sin has nothing to do with how we love one another—any more than how we treat people who eat shellfish or pork, wear mixed fabrics or trim their beards (all laws from the Bible). We can each hold our beliefs and still love one another. The two do not have to be mutually exclusive.

2. **Homosexuality is not a sin.** Throughout the course of my life I've known many men and women in the LGBTQ+ community. Some of them have been open about their sexuality. Many have not been. For much of my life, I also understood homosexuality to be a sin. It's what I'd been taught in church. In my reading of the Bible, it's what I understood. Understanding it as a sin didn't change my love for these men and women. If I'm totally honest, I hadn't put a whole lot of thought into whether it should. Shame on me, because it was important to them.

It's not my goal to change your mind about whether homosexuality is a sin or not. Through study and with the help of a lot of smart theologians, I have changed my perspective on this important topic. If you haven't already, I encourage you to also take another look at your understanding of homosexuality in the Bible. There are a lot of great resources that examine this topic in really thoughtful ways. I hope when you finish this book, you will take the time to look at some of those with an open mind. Here's a place where you can find some: Reformation Project. (reformationproject.org/resources/)

Honestly though, the best way to start reexamining your approach to homosexuality is to open your hearts and doors to people from the gay community. When you worship with them, pray with them, share life with them, you will discover your common ground.

You will find that you're not really that much different. You will come to know them as full people—Christians who are husbands, wives, parents, doctors, teachers, bankers, musicians, artists, gardeners, bakers, readers, writers, oh and a part of the LGBTQ+ community.

It becomes difficult NOT to see LGBTQ+ as fully loved and created children of God when you actually get to know them.

Over recent years, as I've listened to more and more stories from people in the LGBTQ+ community, I am ashamed of the church. We've treated these brothers and sisters poorly. At the very least, we've made them feel unwelcome. At the worst, we've told them God doesn't love them.

I've lost track of the number of times I've sat across the table from gay, bi, trans, Christian people with deep faith and biblical knowledge, who are worried about their own salvation. They've read all of the books and articles that debunk the biblical interpretation of homosexuality as a sin. Yet, they still have a hard time believing it. That's on us as Christians who have allowed them to feel unloved and unwelcome. It breaks my heart.

As I've heard their stories, I've also been inspired to a deeper faith. They've been rejected and ejected from the church. But they haven't rejected God. They have a hunger to know God and be in a relationship with God that I envy. Their faith has been tested in ways I can't imagine. But they haven't given up.

In 1970, Maddy Isaacson, the mother of two, and Sandy Schuster, the mother of four, met at a Pentecostal church in Seattle. When they fell in love and vowed "a covenant with God" to each other, their church forced them out. About that same time, the fathers of their children sued for full custody.

The fathers nearly won. But Maddy and Sandy took their fight all the way to the Seattle Supreme Court which ruled that they could retain custody of their children. This became one of the nation's first legal victories for lesbian or gay parents.

Miss Maddy came into my life about 12 years ago when I started singing at Citichurch. Sandy, her lifelong partner, had passed away a few years earlier. Their children have grown and started their own families.

Miss Maddy doesn't talk a lot about the time when she had to fight for her children or was kicked out of the church because she fell in love with another woman. What she does talk about a lot is her faith in Jesus. Nothing—not rejection, not loss, not struggles, not death—could cause Miss Maddy's faith to waiver.

To even suggest to her the possibility that she might be bitter or question God gets a quiet chuckle, a small shake of her head, and a sweet voice saying, "Oh no sweetie. It's my faith in Jesus that has given me the strength to overcome those things."

I don't know if I've ever known anyone whose faith runs as deeply through their veins as Miss Maddy. Not in spite of all that she's been through, but in many ways because of it. Miss Maddy is one of the people God has placed in my life who constantly inspires me to a deeper faith.

We are all misfits in one way or another. God puts us in each other's lives for a reason. When we recognize that we don't have it figured out any more than the misfit next door, we can build the community of faith that Christ envisioned when he gathered his group of 12 misfits together.

Then, when someone asks how you can associate with *those* people, you can say, "Blame it on Jesus."

As I close this chapter, I want to point out one other thing we can learn from Jesus' gathering of misfits. His message of love was a threat to the religious leaders of the time. When you start to share a true message of unconditional love and welcome the misfits into your fold, the critics will begin to surface. In the next chapter, we will take a look at how we face those critics.

Chapter 3
FACE THE CRITICS

"Your mother would be disappointed in you."

Betty, one of my mom's old friends, had seen a Facebook post I'd made during Gay Pride month. It had been an affirming post claiming God's love for ALL people. Yes...she told me my mother would be disappointed in me for proclaiming God's love.

Betty and I both loved my mother and since my mom had died a few years earlier, she was someone I stayed in touch with as a person who helped keep the memory of my mother alive for me. She was an important person in my life.

So when she said to me, "Your mother would be disappointed in you," it made me stop—for just a second.

My mother, Merle Conn Longnecker, was almost 50 years old when I was born. She was from a different generation than the parents of most of the other kids I grew up with. I had brothers who were 17 and 18 years older than me.

Mom was also a gospel music singer. She was the first woman inducted into the Texas Gospel Music Hall of Fame. The Southern Gospel Music world is filled with people from all different walks of faith. I was exposed to a broad perspective of Christian beliefs growing up in this world.

But always, my faith was founded and centered by the faith of my parents. From them I understood that while there might be a lot of ways we thought about and understood our faith, it was always based on the love shown by Jesus Christ.

The more I connect with and stand up for some of the misfits in my life—the people who haven't always felt welcome by others—the more people feel free to criticize my decisions. And strangely enough, it often comes from some of those people who knew Mom and Dad through their involvement in gospel music.

When I was younger, if someone had said something I didn't understand about my faith, I would have gone to Mom or Dad and asked them about it. And always, it would be seen through the lens of Jesus' love.

I'm no longer surprised when someone I know and care about reaches out to me and tells me in one way or another that Mom or Dad would be disappointed in me. I know how my parents would feel about the direction of my ministry. I know that they would stand right beside me and love like Jesus loved.

It's funny because as I've moved from music ministry into pastoral ministry, more people criticize me about becoming a female pastor than they do for loving LGBTQ+ people. That may be a good sign for gay people.

As more people begin to recognize that their own families include gay people, it becomes more and more difficult for them to stand against people in the LGBTQ+ community. At least some people become less vocally hateful, even if they don't become more vocally supportive.

It's probably not a good sign for the status of women in the world. As far as we've come, it is still popular to target women in authority and women in ministry.

Challenging the Norms

Over the past few years, I have become more vocal about the misfits in my life. This is where my life's journey has led me. Every Sunday, in our Crosswalk worship community at Lovers Lane United Methodist Church, I preach a message of love and acceptance for ALL people. It's a message I believe ALL people need to hear. There's not one among us who hasn't at some point in our life worried that we've done something to exclude ourselves from God's love.

We've seen Crosswalk grow with people who need to hear this message. The misfits of society. The people who haven't always felt welcome in church or other places.

Alcoholics. Divorced women. Gay men and women. Trans people. Drug addicts. Women in leadership. People of color. And the families of people in these communities who want to find a place where their children, parents, brothers and sisters will be welcome.

As unbelievable as this is to me, the more I stand up for the misfits, the more some "people of faith" will tell me I'm making a mistake. They will quote scripture to me to explain why these people will be rejected by God and not be welcomed into the gates of heaven.

The Critics Will Come

This is what you need to know. As you begin to challenge the norms of what people have always believed, what they have been taught by their families and their pastors, and what has shaped the way they've always treated other people—when you challenge these things, *people will stand against you.*

In many ways, I understand this. It's natural to be resistant when someone challenges your way of life. That's what we're talking about. When you tell someone that you believe God loves gay people, that challenges their whole belief system. Their whole lives, they've been taught that that isn't true.

Even if this particular challenge hasn't impacted them directly—they're not gay, no one in their family is (openly) gay, they've only been acquainted with gay people in distant ways—it has allowed them to develop a world view about LGBTQ+ people that is built around fear, dismissiveness, and condescension.

On one hand it may not be that they have actively treated gay people poorly, they just haven't thought about them at all. On the other hand it may have given them permission to treat gay, lesbian, or trans people they've met badly. Maybe they've chosen a straight, less qualified person to hire for a job. Maybe they've refused to do business with a same-sex couple. Or maybe they've gone so far as to join in on some good old-fashioned gay-bashing.

You can replace "gay" with any other word that describes the misfits in our lives—lesbian, alcoholic, divorcee, trans, drug addict, woman, black, immigrant...the list goes on and on.

No one wants to be told their wrong. If they have to accept this "new" truth, what other truth will they have to accept next? What other ways of thinking will they have to adjust? To change? Nobody likes change. So when you stand up for what you believe, be prepared for people to resist.

Learning From Your Critics

Here's the thing. I've come to be OK with people who question me. I've learned to be grateful for people who question me. People who question me or who think I'm doing something wrong are the exact people I want to talk to! No one's perspective on the world has ever changed without talking to people who disagree with them.

I have grown in my faith because of people who disagree with me. It doesn't mean I always change my mind on a topic—though sometimes I might. But it does mean, at the very least I come away from the conversation with a better understanding of another perspective.

I can have compassion for another's way of thinking and still not agree with them. I can have respect for them as a child of God and still stand up for those their position harms.

What would the world be like if we all agreed on everything? We would still all think the world is flat. Flat earthers believe the Earth is not round. Some even base their beliefs on biblical passages like "the four corners of the Earth" (Isaiah 11:12 KJV) or a "a firmament in the midst of the waters" (Genesis 1:6 KJV), which they understand to be a literal description of a flat, dome-covered world.

With a logical explanation of why we never fall off the edge, *most* people eventually came to see the truth without compromising their faith.

We can never expect to change the minds of everyone. There are still flat earthers today! People don't want to be told they're wrong. Sometimes, no matter what you say, they're not going to be on the same page as you. We can still love them. That's what Jesus would do.

Facing Your Critics

Jesus certainly faces his critics. Jesus comes to shake things up. He challenges an established way of life for the Jews and the Gentiles. He tells people they are wrong. He speaks and eats with the misfits of the time. It was inevitable that he too would be held up to critique.

When Jesus dines with Matthew, it is a moment that shakes the religious establishment. Matthew is a tax collector—a profession that makes him one of the most despised people among the Jews. Tax collectors are seen as traitors, working for the occupying Roman government and often cheating their fellow Jews out of money. So when Jesus calls Matthew to follow him and then goes to Matthew's house for a meal, it is a bold move.

Matthew invites many of his friends, fellow tax collectors, and others who are considered sinners, to join them for dinner. This isn't the kind of crowd that religious leaders of the time associate with. The Pharisees, who are strict about following religious laws and keeping themselves pure, are appalled. They believe that associating with sinners will make you spiritually unclean. Jesus is gaining a reputation as a respected teacher. So seeing him sitting down to eat with these people upsets the Pharisees.

"HEALTHY PEOPLE DON'T NEED A DOCTOR, BUT SICK PEOPLE DO."

Luke 5:31

They see this as more than just bad company. It challenges their entire way of thinking about righteousness. They focus on strict adherence to the law and separating themselves from those they deem unworthy. Here is Jesus, seeming to reject their approach entirely, choosing instead to spend time with the very people the Pharisees won't even speak to.

When they question Jesus about it, his response cuts to the heart of the matter. He tells them, "Healthy people don't need a doctor, but sick people do. I didn't come to call righteous people but sinners to change their hearts and lives" (Luke 5:31-32).

Mission of Mercy

Jesus makes it clear that his mission comes from mercy, not maintaining a facade of religious superiority. He is more interested in reaching out to those who know they need help than in reinforcing the Pharisees' sense of self-righteousness.

Even in the face of his critics Jesus goes to those on the margins, those who are rejected by society, and calls them to a life with God. It is a radical departure from the way the Pharisees practice their faith, and it upsets their entire worldview.

Like Jesus, when we reach out to those who are overlooked or judged harshly by society, our critics will question our choices. They will say we're associating with the "wrong" kind of people or that we're not being careful enough about our reputation.

I can't get over the irony that in our rush to judgment, we forget that we are all sinners. We all need the same forgiveness, yet we feel free to highlight the sins of others as "worse" than our own. Jesus shows us that love, grace, and mercy are far more important than worrying about what others think.

Critics will always be there, especially when you step outside the boundaries of what's considered "acceptable." But Jesus doesn't let that stop him. He knows his mission is to bring healing and forgiveness to those who need it most, regardless of what the self-righteous think.

Biblical Bullies

Today, the Bible remains a powerful source of inspiration and guidance for millions. Yet, it has also been weaponized to justify acts of injustice and to justify critics of progress in our effort to love ALL people. People will use scripture to "prove" to you that you have turned on your faith.

Racial Equality: The legacy of slavery may be in the past, but we still feel its echoes in the form of systemic racism. Some still hold on to biblical passages that were once used to justify slavery, twisting their meanings to support modern-day racial intolerance.

These interpretations overlook the Bible's deeper message of unity in Christ, where, as Paul writes, "There is neither Jew nor Greek; there is neither slave nor free; nor is there male and female, for you are all one in Christ Jesus" (Galatians 3:28). Still, these ancient justifications have left a stain on how race is perceived and discussed, subtly and directly influencing attitudes that perpetuate inequality and discrimination.

Women's Rights: Women have faced ongoing struggles against scripture that has been used to justify their oppression. In some religious communities, women are still not allowed to preach, denied leadership roles, or relegated to traditional, subservient positions. They focus on interpretations of verses that emphasize submission, yet they ignore the broader biblical narrative that includes strong, influential women like

Deborah, Esther, and Mary Magdalene. The Bible also teaches that in Christ, "there is no male and female" (Galatians 3:28), emphasizing equality in the eyes of God.

Anti-Semitism: Certain passages, particularly those related to the crucifixion of Jesus, have been twisted to blame Jewish people for his death, fueling hatred and violence. This interpretation has persisted today, contributing to a recent resurgence of anti-Semitic rhetoric and actions. Jesus himself taught us to "Love your enemies and pray for those who persecute you" (Matthew 5:44), a directive that contradicts the hatred often justified by a misreading of scripture.

LGBTQ Rights: We've talked about the use of the Bible in debates over LGBTQ+ rights. Those who oppose the rights of LGBTQ+ individuals cite verses from Leviticus or Romans as a moral shield to defend their exclusionary ways. The pain inflicted by these misinterpretations of scripture is profound, leading to discrimination, rejection, and violence.

When taken out of context or selectively interpreted, scripture can be wielded as a tool for oppression rather than a source of liberation. The very text meant to unite us in love and justice is used to justify injustice in the name of righteousness.

This is not just a theological issue. It's also a social one, with real consequences for how we live together in a world that desperately needs more compassion, understanding, and unity. To move forward, we must reclaim the Bible's true message, using it to break down barriers rather than build them, and to seek justice and love in all that we do. Remember the command to "do justice, embrace faithful love, and walk humbly with your God" (Micah 6:8).

The Irony of Perfection

These barriers set an expectation that perfection is required for acceptance by God. Christ's message never requires perfection to be welcome into the church—let alone God's realms.

Paul has a lot to say about the idea of perfection, but he approaches it in a way that recognizes we're all human and far from flawless. He encourages believers to aim high—to strive for a life that looks more and more like Christ. But he also understands the challenge to achieve it.

In his letter to the Philippians, Paul admits that he hasn't reached perfection himself. He says, "I myself don't think I've reached it, but I do this one thing: I forget about the things behind me and reach out for the things ahead of me. The goal I pursue is the prize of God's upward call in Christ Jesus" (Philippians 3:13-14). For Paul, the Christian life is about progress, not perfection. It is a journey of growth, with the goal to become more like Jesus, even if that means stumbling along the way.

Paul also makes it clear that our perfection isn't something we can achieve on our own. He talks about presenting believers as "fully mature" in Christ (Colossians 2:6). That word "mature" could also mean "perfect," but the idea isn't to be flawless—it's to grow into the person God wants us to be, with Jesus at the center.

Paul understands that everyone falls short. He says it clearly, "all have sinned and fall short of God's glory" (Romans 3:23). That's Paul's way of reminding us that no one is perfect and that it's okay because our righteousness doesn't come from being perfect—it comes from faith in Jesus. Paul knows we all need grace. He says God told him, "My grace is enough for you, because power is made perfect in weakness" (2 Corinthians 12:9). Instead of hiding his weaknesses, Paul embraces them, because that's where God's power shows up the most.

THE CHRISTIAN LIFE IS ABOUT PROGRESS, NOT PERFECTION.

When Paul talks about perfection, he isn't setting up an impossible standard. He is encouraging believers to keep growing, to keep moving forward, and to rely on God's grace when they fall short. Perfection isn't about being without fault. It is about being complete and mature in Christ, always pressing on in the journey of faith.

The irony of Jesus not expecting perfection from us yet offering unconditional love is one of the most beautiful and profound aspects of his message. It flips the usual way we think about relationships on its head.

Perfect Love

In our everyday lives, love often feels conditional. We're used to thinking that we have to earn love by being good enough, smart enough, or successful enough. But Jesus redefines that notion. He knows we're imperfect—he knows we'll make mistakes, struggle with doubts, and sometimes fail. Yet, he doesn't wait for us to get our act together before he loves us. His love isn't something we earn by being perfect. It's a gift he gives freely, no strings attached.

In a world that often tells us we need to be perfect to be loved, Jesus loves us just as we are. Given freely and without conditions, this love has the power to transform us. It's the ultimate irony: we don't have to be perfect to be loved perfectly.

CS Lewis said, "Though our feelings come and go, His love for us does not. It is not wearied by our sins, or our indifference; and therefore, it is quite relentless in its determination that we shall be cured of those sins, at whatever cost to us, at whatever cost to him."

IT'S THE ULTIMATE IRONY: WE DON'T HAVE TO BE PERFECT TO BE LOVED PERFECTLY.

The irony lies in the fact that while we might think we need to be perfect to deserve love, Jesus loves us fully, even in our imperfection. He doesn't set a bar to leap over before we can be worthy of his love. Instead, he meets us right where we are, flaws and all, and loves us anyway. His unconditional love is what makes us want to strive to be better—not because we have to earn his love, but because his love inspires us to grow and become more like him.

Ruffling Feathers

When we start to embrace this idea that Christ loves us flaws and all, and when we start to teach that Jesus' message of love trumps any other messages, some of our brothers and sisters of the faith get their feathers ruffled.

That's just what happens. Sometimes people will agree with what we have to say about loving ALL people, in principle. But when you get specific and challenge a rule, or law, or scripture they hold dear, they find a way to hold it above these basic tenets of love. Or even worse, to use their rule to justify straight-up hate—all in the name of Jesus.

It's not always easy to understand, but I remind myself that in some ways, I was once in that camp. Though I truly believe I never justified bigotry, there were times when I stood by and allowed it to happen. Even with the lessons of love and acceptance I learned from my parents, I had to come to my own understanding of how to balance these ideals of Jesus with other teachings of accountability I'd learned from others.

I'm grateful that through study of new and old theologians, by listening to the voices of people who agree and disagree with me, by meeting and befriending the people who are most impacted by these Bible-bashing scriptures, and by following the lead of the Holy Spirit—through all of these I have come to fully embrace Christ's message of love. I can now hear these scriptures in the context that they were written or in a way that I can respond to God's grace in my own life—not as a condition for receiving God's grace.

Through that understanding, I have found myself compelled to be more vocal in my support of the misfits who have accepted me and all of my flaws into their lives. With that comes the old "friends" who tell me my mother would be disappointed.

Jesus and His Critics

Jesus handled criticism with a combination of wisdom, compassion, and firmness. He says, "Bless those who curse you. Pray for those who mistreat you" (Luke 6:28). Uh oh. That's a hard one. Straight from the Jesus files, here are some lessons we can learn about how to do that.

1. **Respond with Questions:** Often, Jesus answers criticism by asking questions that prompt self-reflection. When religious leaders criticize him for healing on the Sabbath, he asks them if it is lawful to do good on the Sabbath (Mark 3:1-6). His question leaves them speechless. Asking thoughtful questions can force our critics to close their mouths. It doesn't always mean they will walk away agreeing with you. They certainly don't agree with Jesus. But it might give you space to move forward.

2. **Use the Teaching Moments:** Jesus uses criticism as opportunities to teach deeper truths. When called out for breaking the law by picking grain on the Sabbath, he responds by reminding them of David eating the consecrated bread when he is hungry and how priests work on the Sabbath without being guilty. He says, "I want mercy and not sacrifice" (Matthew 12:7). He uses their critique to teach about the heart of the law, prioritizing

compassion and mercy over legalistic rule-keeping. We can turn criticism into a moment to share our values and perspectives, helping others to understand our motivations and beliefs more clearly.

3. **Silence:** Sometimes, Jesus chooses not to respond at all. During his trial, when the chief priests and elders accuse him, he remains silent, fulfilling the prophecy of Isaiah (Matthew 26:62-63). I have to confess, this lesson might be the hardest for me. But there are times when silence is the best response, especially when the criticism is unjust or when engaging will only make the situation worse.

4. **Correct Misunderstandings:** Jesus corrects misunderstandings directly but with grace. When Martha is upset that Mary was not helping her, Jesus gently points out that Mary has chosen the better part by listening to his teaching (Luke 10:38-42). When we find ourselves in the middle of a misunderstanding, we can follow Jesus' example by clarifying the situation calmly and kindly, helping others see the bigger picture.

5. **Challenge Hypocrisy:** Jesus doesn't shy away from calling out hypocrisy. He openly criticizes the Pharisees and teachers of the law for their outward display of piety while neglecting justice and love (Matthew 23). When we encounter hypocrisy, we can address it directly, but always with respect and humility, recognizing we all live with some sort of hypocrisy in our lives. Addressing it can help build integrity and honesty in our rela-

tionships and communities.

6. **Forgive:** At the heart of Jesus' ministry is forgiveness. Even in the face of severe criticism and suffering, Jesus exemplifies this virtue. On the cross, he prays for those who crucified him, saying, "Father, forgive them, for they don't know what they're doing" (Luke 23:34). Embracing forgiveness, even when we've been wronged, frees us from bitterness and allows us to move forward with peace and compassion.

If we're doing it right, we are all going to have our own Pharisees—people who want to hold the laws above people. But Jesus calls us to love people more than the rules.

A couple of years ago, I was leading the music at the funeral of a prominent woman named Lydia at a large church in Fort Worth. I'd known this woman and her family for many years. She was a loving and kind woman who always had good things to say to me. I had sung with her and her family on many stages over the years.

Lydia's family was filled with great musicians and singers, so I accepted the invitation to be part of her funeral as a great honor. When I arrived, I met one of her sons who welcomed me graciously. We gathered with everyone else who would have a role in the service. The man who would preach, the man who would read the scripture, the man who would share a story about the mother, the man who would read another scripture, the man who would welcome everyone to the service and me, the woman who would sing the song. Other than me, everyone with a role in the service was a man.

Shortly before the service, we were all standing on the raised platform as the pastor began directing the worship participants to our seats. When everyone else had been seated in the chairs on the platform, he pointed to the first pew on the floor, and said, "We've got a seat for you right down there." I looked from the top of the stage, down what seemed like a stack of 50 steps to the floor and saw my seat.

Honestly, this didn't surprise me. I'd been in many churches over the years as the featured singer or even doing my own concert where the pastor and the leaders would retire to the pastor's office to pray before the service began. But because I was a woman, I wasn't invited.

This was the way it was. The way it still is in many churches. People have an idea of other's place in the world and they won't be moved from it. The Pharisees in my life have always pushed me to the back—until they wanted me to sing for them.

At this particular funeral, I opened the service with the first song. As the pastor made the welcome, I climbed the mountain of steps and stood ready to sing. When I finished my song, the man on the last seat of the row got up to read the scripture or the obituary or whatever came next in the service.

As the man and I passed each other on the platform, I saw the open seat he had just left. It was the last chair at the end of the row on the platform. I walked to the chair and sat down. I'm not going to lie. I experienced a little pleasure when the man finished his reading, turned from the pulpit and, with the slightest look of surprise, saw me sitting where he had been sitting before. He paused slightly as he passed to walk down the long flight of stairs to take *his* seat in the front pew of the Sanctuary.

When we step out of our comfort zones, people are going to talk. When we challenge the way people think by our words, people are going to get uncomfortable. When we flaunt God's love in ways they don't understand it, people are going to get upset.

When your critics come after you for the way you love, they become a lot easier to face when you remember to "Blame it on Jesus."

A good friend of mine, Rev. Kennon Pickett, recently said this, "The truth is, not all criticism is worth your time and energy. Remember, if you wouldn't seek advice from someone, their criticism should hold little weight in your heart."

Ultimately, I think that's the bottom line. Knowing who to listen to and which battles to fight play an important role in our efforts to fight hate with love. In the next chapter, we're going to talk about what we can learn from Jesus about picking our battles.

Chapter 4
PICK YOUR BATTLES

M Y MOM WAS A gospel singer who spent years touring the country, living the life of the road. If there was a gospel group out there, she knew them, loved them, and looked out for them. That's why people called her "Mama Merle." She wasn't just a singer. She was a caretaker, always ready to help people she cared about.

This life wasn't glamorous. The gospel groups traveled in buses, staying in roadside motels along the way. And just like any group of people, they had their struggles, their own demons to fight. They were real people, with real problems, just like you and me.

One night, long before I was born, Mom was jolted awake by a noise outside the motel. It was the middle of the night, but there was a crowd gathering on the sidewalk. Curious and concerned, she threw on her robe and stepped out to see what was going on.

As she got closer, she saw a man lying in the middle of the highway, moaning in pain. It didn't take her long to recognize him. It was Oscar, a singer with one of the gospel groups on tour. Oscar had a problem with alcohol, though not many people knew it. Mom did. He was a brilliant songwriter with a baritone voice that could bring you to tears. Oscar loved Jesus deeply, but sometimes, the bottle had a stronger hold on him than his faith.

Mom looked around at the crowd on the sidewalk. They were just standing there, whispering, pointing fingers, but not one of them made a move to help. It was like they were frozen in place, just watching as Oscar lay drunk in the road.

My mom knew all the Bible verses those people were thinking of as they stood there. She knew how they might justify their inaction with scriptures that warn against drunkenness or associating with "drunkards." And she'd heard whole sermons warning about what would happen if she associated with "drunkards."

OSCAR LOVED JESUS DEEPLY, BUT SOMETIMES, THE BOTTLE HAD A STRONGER HOLD ON HIM THAN HIS FAITH.

But Mom also knew that Jesus told us to "love your neighbor as yourself." And Oscar wasn't just some neighbor. He was a friend. So while everyone else stood on that sidewalk, glued to the ground by their judgment, she stepped out and walked to Oscar.

When she reached him, he looked up at her, eyes filled with tears. He was broken, lost in his struggle, and ashamed. But Mama Merle didn't hesitate. She told him it was time to get up and go back to his room. He kept crying, lying in the street. She knelt down beside him and prayed. Then with all the strength she could muster, helped him to his feet and walked him back to his room.

As they passed by, the others looked on in shock and disdain. They couldn't believe she was helping him. But Mom didn't care. She knew what needed to be done, and she did it. She didn't wait for approval; she just acted out of love.

Life is full of moments when we have to choose between standing on the sidelines, watching, judging, or stepping up and doing what's right, even when it's hard. It's easy to get caught up in what others think, to worry about how we'll be perceived. But sometimes, we have to push all that aside and just do what needs to be done.

How do we know when those times are?

Doing God's Will

When we think about the phrase "picking your battles," it's easy to imagine a wise person who knows when to speak up and when to let things slide. Interestingly, Jesus models this idea throughout his life and ministry. He doesn't try to get caught up in every little argument or conflict that comes his way. Instead, he demonstrates a keen sense of when to engage and when to step back, all while keeping his focus on what truly matters: Doing God's will, focusing on the greater good, and engaging with purpose.

Prioritizing God's Will

First and foremost, Jesus prioritizes doing the will of God above everything else. He knows his mission on earth is to fulfill God's plan, not to get bogged down by every dispute or challenge others bring his way.

When Satan tempts Jesus with challenges in the wilderness and tries to get him to prove his power or to satisfy his own needs, Jesus doesn't take the bait (Matthew 4:1-11). He knows that engaging in a power struggle with Satan isn't part of his mission. Instead, he stays true to God's will by responding with scripture. He didn't need to prove anything to Satan.

Then there is the time Jesus is asked to settle a dispute over an inheritance (Luke 12:13-15). Instead of getting caught up in a family feud, he redirects the conversation to teach a lesson about greed and the dangers of focusing on material wealth. Jesus recognizes that some battles simply aren't worth fighting because they don't align with his primary mission of revealing God's kingdom.

Focusing on the Greater Good

Jesus focuses on the greater good by keeping his eye on the issues that have a lasting impact on people's lives and spiritual well-being. He doesn't waste time on trivial matters. The religious leaders criticize him for breaking the Sabbath law, but Jesus sees the bigger picture. He understands that healing a person in need is far more important than rigidly following the rules.

When he heals the man with the withered hand, Jesus challenges the leaders by asking, "Is it legal on the Sabbath to do good or to do evil, to save life or to kill?" (Mark 3:1-6). By focusing on the greater good—helping and healing—Jesus shows that some battles are worth engaging in, especially when they align with God's heart for mercy and compassion.

When Jesus feeds the 5,000 (John 6:1-14), he doesn't get frustrated with the disciples' lack of resources. He focuses on the greater good—feeding a hungry crowd. He doesn't engage in a debate about how impossible the situation seems. He acts with purpose, multiplying the loaves and fishes to meet the needs of the people. Jesus isn't interested in arguing over what can't be done. He is focused on what should be done.

Engaging with Purpose

Jesus is intentional about engaging with purpose. He doesn't shy away from confrontation when it is necessary, but he always has a clear reason for the battles he takes on. When he clears the temple, Jesus doesn't go on a rampage just to prove a point. He is defending the sanctity of God's house. The temple has become a marketplace, and Jesus knows this is a battle worth fighting because it strikes at the core of true worship and reverence for God (Matthew 21:12-13).

Any time Jesus confronts the Pharisees and teachers of the law, he does so with a purpose—to expose their hypocrisy and to call them back to true righteousness (Matthew 23). Jesus doesn't engage in these battles to win arguments or to show off his wisdom. He does it to challenge systems of injustice and to bring people closer to God.

Tilting at Windmills

"Tilting at windmills" is an old metaphor that comes from the classic book *Don Quixote* by Miguel de Cervantes. While de Cervantes didn't use this exact phrase, it beautifully sums up a scene where the main character, Don Quixote, mistakes windmills for dangerous giants and charges at them with his lance. This act of "tilting"—which means jousting—against these misunderstood windmills describes what it's like to chase after pointless or misguided efforts.

Our battle to fight hate with love is too important for us to waste our time tilting at windmills.

Today, when people think about Christians, they often think more about what we're against than what we stand for. This may be the result of our brothers and sisters who focus on sticking to the letter of the Bible without catching its spirit. They get so wrapped up in the details that they miss out on its big, beautiful picture. This focus on rules can put us at risk of losing our personal connections with God and each other.

Focusing on the strict standards of our faith can lead to judgment and disdain, making Christians seem aloof and insensitive. Plus, believing we can live up to the "rules" perfectly will leave us feeling guilty and anxious, draining all the joy and peace our faith is meant to bring.

It can create the belief that we have to earn our way into heaven with good deeds rather than accepting it as the free gift of grace it is. This old-school legalism clings to the outdated Bible interpretations we've talked about, ignoring the context in which scripture was written.

TODAY, WHEN PEOPLE THINK ABOUT CHRISTIANS, THEY OFTEN THINK MORE ABOUT WHAT WE'RE AGAINST THAN WHAT WE STAND FOR.

Paul's letters tackle this head-on. Paul writes about moving from old Jewish laws, like circumcision, to a new kind of faith built on the grace of Jesus Christ. He makes it clear that those old rules aren't necessary anymore because Jesus' sacrifice brought us freedom and grace instead of a checklist of rules.

A Modern Approach to Scripture

Today, our challenge is to honor the Bible's teachings while living out the love, freedom, and grace Jesus offers. How do we let the Bible guide our moral and spiritual life without turning it into a tool for judgment? The key is understanding the Bible's historical and cultural setting and focusing more on its key messages of love, grace, and redemption.

As Christians, we're called to live by the Bible's teachings. But it's crucial not to fall into picking battles based on old judgmental habits. We must listen to leaders and teachers who help us understand the Bible in its true context. The Bible wasn't intended to be a rule book, but to guide our relationship with God and one another. With this understanding, we can focus our efforts on love, grace, and redemption and live out the compassion and love that Jesus showed us.

The Importance of Context

The Bible was written thousands of years ago, in societies vastly different from ours. The cultural norms, societal structures, and historical events that shaped the lives of biblical characters were specific to their time and place. When we read the Bible without considering this context, we risk misinterpreting its messages or applying its teachings in ways that were never intended.

Many of the laws in the Old Testament are given to the Israelites in a specific context—an ancient, nomadic society striving to survive and maintain its identity amid surrounding pagan cultures. If taken out of context, some of these laws can seem harsh or outdated. But when we understand that these laws are meant to set the Israelites of the time apart and preserve their relationship with God, we can appreciate their purpose without needing to apply them literally to our modern lives.

The same is true of the New Testament letters. The authors of those letters write them for early Christian communities facing unique challenges, from persecution to internal divisions. Paul's letters, for example, often address specific issues within these communities, and his advice is tailored to their circumstances. Without this understanding, we tend to take his words out of context, and apply them literally to our lives today.

Focusing on the Core Messages

While context is crucial, it's also essential to focus on the Bible's core messages—those timeless truths that transcend culture and history. The messages of love, grace, and redemption are at the heart of the Christian faith. These are the principles that Jesus emphasizes throughout his ministry, and they should guide our interpretation of the entire Bible.

Jesus repeatedly teaches that love is the greatest commandment. He summarizes the entire law with two commands: to love God and to love our neighbors as ourselves (Matthew 22:37-40). This love is not limited to those who think, act, or believe as we do. It extends to everyone, including those we might be tempted to judge.

My dear friend, Maddy Isaacson, taught me the phrase "Extra Grace Required." We all have difficult people in our lives who need a little "EGR." When we remember that we are all flawed and in need of grace—an undeserved favor that we did nothing to earn—it'a a whole lot easier to give a little EGR to others, even when they fall short of our expectations.

Redemption is the ultimate hope offered through Jesus. No matter how far someone has strayed, no one is beyond the reach of God's redemptive power. This should encourage us to see others through the lens of love, grace, and redemption rather than judgment, understanding that everyone has the potential for transformation through Christ.

The Danger of Intolerance

Discounting the Bible's context or losing sight of its core messages, creates space for intolerance to creep in. We might start to view ourselves as moral gatekeepers, determining who is "in" and who is "out" based on our interpretations. This harms our relationships and misrepresents the heart of the Christian faith.

WHEN WE FOCUS ON CONDEMNING OTHERS RATHER THAN EXTENDING LOVE AND GRACE, WE BECOME STUMBLING BLOCKS RATHER THAN BRIDGES TO CHRIST.

Judgmental attitudes will drive people away from the church and God. It defeats the whole purpose of the church! When we focus on condemning others rather than extending love and grace, we become stumbling blocks rather than bridges to Christ. Jesus reserves his harshest criticism not for sinners, but for the religious leaders who were quick to judge and slow to show mercy.

We Might Be Wrong

Here's the thing. We might not be right about every stand we take. History is scattered with people who died on their swords to defend an idea they were convinced was true. At one time people thought that bathing was bad for you. They thought that opening the pores of the skin in warm water would lead to disease. I wonder if they believed in perfume!

Less than 100 years ago, tobacco was advertised as healthy and widely believed to be a stress reliever and weight-loss aid. Of course, we now know the devastating effects of tobacco, including heart disease and cancer.

And let's not forget those flat-earthers.

The point is, we have to approach our battles with the understanding that we might not always have it exactly right. With that kind of humility, we open the door to listen to other people's perspectives. We expand the size of our tent when we present ourselves as welcoming. And we might even learn something new.

When we listen to others, they are much more likely to listen to us. We can't open doors to conversation by standing on our bully pulpit and pointing out the perceived flaws in everyone else. It just doesn't work. You've probably been on the receiving end of that kind of conversation. Nobody wants that.

People Over Rules

Several years ago, Rev. Clifton Howard, one of the most important mentors in my life, preached a sermon about the woman at the well. You remember her right?

Jesus was passing through Samaria, which was kind of a big deal because Jews and Samaritans back then didn't really get along. They had a lot of history and didn't see eye to eye on religious matters. Side note, some things aren't new.

Jesus, tired from his journey, stops at a well around noon—it is hot at this time of day, and he is worn out. While he's there, a Samaritan woman comes to draw water, which is unusual because women usually go to the well early in the morning or late in the evening to avoid the heat.

Jesus starts a conversation with her by asking for a drink of water. She is surprised because men don't talk to women they don't know, and a Jewish man definitely doesn't ask a Samaritan woman for anything. She says, "Why are you, a Jew, asking me, a Samaritan woman, for water?"

Jesus tells her about this living water he can provide, water that will quench her thirst forever. The woman is intrigued and a bit puzzled, thinking he's talking about actual water, and she says, "Give me this water so I won't be thirsty again, and won't have to come here to draw water."

His conversation with her continues until she sees she has encountered the Messiah. She runs back to her town, leaving her jar behind and tells everyone she met about Jesus.

WHEN RULES GIVE US THE AUTHORITY TO FORCE PEOPLE TO GO TO THE WELL BY THEMSELVES IN THE HEAT OF THE DAY, WE'VE MISSED THE POINT.

Pastor Clifton finished his sermon saying, "Jesus knew the rules. But Jesus also knew the woman at the well. He knew that this woman was more important than the rules."

Pastor Clifton remains an important mentor in my life, but that lesson from him that day has stuck with me more clearly than any other. It didn't hurt that it came from a man who I'd seen live out this kind of compassion time and time again. Jeff even wrote it down on one of the pew prayer cards and has it hanging on a bulletin board to this day.

When we get so focused on the rules, we often miss the actual needs of the person standing right in front of us. Rules are important. They provide order to our world. But people are more important. When rules give us the authority to force people to go to the well by themselves in the heat of the day, we've missed the point. We are in danger of weaponizing scripture to justify our prejudice and hate.

Becoming Pharisees

When we justify our exclusion of other people on the understanding of the rules, our vision may be distorted by the log in our own eyes. Any battle we approach will always be impacted by the biases of our personal experiences, the parents who raised us, the communities we live in, our politics, our race, our gender. The list goes on and on.

So too will be the stand people take against us. It's easy to demonize the people we disagree with. They just don't understand. How can they be so ignorant?

But the more confident we get in fighting our battles, the more potential there is for us to become the very Pharisees we fight.

But DeDe, you say, we *are* right!

I have a friend, Larry. He is a great guy. He's kind. He's loving. He has a deep passion for ensuring that all people have equal access to wealth, opportunities, and privileges of society. This commitment to social justice is rooted in the concept that everyone deserves to live in a fair and just society. He supports LGBTQ+ causes, ending homelessness, equality for women, fighting global warming. Not only does he talk passionately about any of these topics, but he also actively works to bring justice to the subjects he believes in.

Honestly, I am envious of his passion. He exudes confidence in his beliefs.

But at the same time his confidence can be off-putting and intimidating. He's all-in and wants everyone else to be all-in. Larry has a unique ability to turn almost any conversation to the injustices of the world and how we should be working to fix them.

You probably have a Larry in your life. You feel like you have to watch every word you say. If you comment on how cute a little girl's new dress is, the conversation may turn to her rights to make decisions about her own body. Or he might tell you that his own children's clothes are all hand-me-downs to help offset the environmental cost of fashion or about the impact her dress leads to child labor in another country.

Hear me when I say, I'm not suggesting that Larry is wrong—or right—in the issues he stands for. On most topics, we find common ground.

What I am saying is that in his attempts to change the world, he can seem very self-righteous and as a result unappealing to the people he is trying to change. Just like the Pharisees become legalistic in their support of the "rules," so too can we in our love for the misfits in our lives.

We have to be confident in the stands we take. But we must be careful about how we take them. The danger is that we become so confident that we become Pharisees of another sort. Not everyone has gotten to the same place where we are. When we remember the journey we've traveled, we can help people. We can walk alongside people on their own journey. In the end that's a whole lot easier than trying to drag them to catch up with us!

Avoiding Intolerance

How can we, as Christians, avoid becoming a part of the problem instead of creating an open, tolerant approach to the challenges of the world. Guess what? Jesus is a great example for how to pick our battles with love and grace.

1. **Seek Understanding Before Judging:** Before forming an opinion about someone else's behavior or beliefs, take the time to understand their context. This might mean learning more about their background, culture, or personal struggles. It also

involves understanding the biblical context of any scriptures you might be tempted to use in judgment. We see this in the story of Jesus meeting the Samaritan woman at the well. He engages her in a deep conversation that addresses not just her personal history but also her cultural and religious context. Jesus looks beyond conventional judgments to understand and minister to her individual needs.

2. **Focus on Our Own Growth:** Jesus warns against trying to remove the speck from your brother's eye while ignoring the plank in your own (Matthew 7:3-5). Focusing on our spiritual growth and our relationship with God first will help us stay humble and less likely to judge others. Jesus encourages a personal journey towards improvement that is mindful of one's own flaws.

3. **Embrace Humility:** Jesus lives a life of humility despite his divine nature, choosing to serve rather than be served. He demonstrates this vividly when he washed his disciples' feet (John 13:1-17). Feet are nasty, y'all. This was a profound lesson in humility, showing that true leadership and relationships are grounded in serving and valuing others. We are all recipients of God's grace, and none of us have it all figured out. Approaching others with humility rather than superiority fosters a more compassionate and understanding attitude.

4. **Prioritize Love:** Jesus demonstrates his own commandment to "love your neighbor as yourself" in every interaction, whether he was healing the sick, forgiving sinners, or teaching his disci-

ples. His response to those who try to trap him with questions about the law consistently reveal a focus on love and mercy over legalism. People have dismissed the "WWJD" movement as trite and oversimplified, but sometimes that's exactly what we need. When in doubt, ask yourself how Jesus would respond in the situation—what would Jesus do? Chances are, he would respond with love, patience, and grace rather than judgment.

5. **Pray for a Heart of Compassion:** Jesus often withdraws to pray, seeking strength and guidance from God. His prayers, especially those that intercede for others as they do just before his arrest, demonstrate his compassion and deep care for humanity (John 17:16-29). He teaches his followers to pray in a way that aligns with God's will, which includes a heart of compassion towards one another. We can ask God to help us see others through his eyes and to give us a heart of compassion. This will transform how we interact with and think about others.

Warning, Warning!

Standing up for what's right won't be easy.

Tom Shipp was the first pastor of Lovers Lane United Methodist Church from 1945 to 1977. He came from another nearby church where he had begun ministering to men who had addictions to alcohol.

This was a time when many people still saw alcoholism as a moral failure or lack of willpower rather than a medical condition. Alcoholics were often viewed as irresponsible, lazy, or weak. Many struggling with alcohol dependency suffered from social isolation, shame, and judgment.

Some of the leadership at his previous church saw the direction Tom's outreach to alcoholics was moving and were happy enough when he accepted the appointment to lead the new up-start church on Lovers Lane. When Tom arrived at his new church, he embraced alcoholics as members of this new church and offered one-on-one counseling to anyone who needed his help.

Even in those early days at Lovers Lane, he met some resistance. When one family decided to go to another church, they said it was because they didn't want to belong to the "First Church of the Alcoholic." But Tom had a heart for these men and refused to be deterred.

Now, forty years later, more than 3,600 people each week find recovery through the Twelfth Step Ministry launched through Lovers Lane United Methodist Church. This ministry provides a place for hope, help, and support in a safe, inclusive environment to the recovery community of North Texas. Thousands of people have found relief from addictions of all kinds because of a legacy started because Tom Shipp insisted on loving ALL people just like Jesus did.

Opening the door to all people isn't easy. Hurt people—people who have been rejected, people who have been turned away, people who have been told they're not good enough, people who have been told God doesn't love them—they come with baggage. Some of them come with a whole U-Haul trailer full of baggage. You've told them you love them and that means you have to love the baggage they bring.

No one said it would be easy. Be prepared for disappointment. Be prepared to be hurt yourself. Years of negative conditioning doesn't just go away just because you've said I love you. Telling them that God loves them doesn't just erase the pain that comes from tears of hearing that God doesn't love them.

They've often built walls of protection around their hearts. Be prepared to chip away at it one a bit at a time. You may one step in their path to truly discovering God's love for them. It may be someone else who helps them get over the finish line.

As I write this, our church is in prayer for a young man who is in ICU after attempting to take his life. He's new to our congregation, but the demons he's fighting are not new. He's testified to feeling accepted for the first time in his life in our church, but his battles are real. The closer he gets to God, the harder some of those demons are set to fight.

Facing Disappointment

Doing the right thing is filled with disappointment. Jesus knew that. Despite being his closest followers, his disciples even disappointed him with their lack of understanding, faith, and commitment.

Peter, James, and John fall asleep in the Garden of Gethsemane instead of keeping watch as Jesus has asked (Matthew 26:40-41). In his moment of deepest anguish, Jesus finds them unable to support him. They just can't grasp the gravity of the situation.

Despite boldly declaring that he would never deny Jesus, Peter does so three times out of fear (Luke 22:54-62). He not only betrays Jesus but also reveals the disciples' struggle with fear and self-preservation over loyalty to their teacher.

The disciples often misunderstand Jesus' teachings, focusing on earthly power rather than spiritual truths. They argue about who among them is the greatest, missing Jesus' message about humility and service (Luke 22:24-26).

Even those closest to Jesus are flawed and human. What did Jesus do? He continues to teach, love, and guide them, embodying the very grace he preaches.

Lifting as We Rise

In her book *The Opposite of Faith*, Nadia Bolz-Weber says, "we aren't being spiritually graded on a curve. There is no table of judges deciding how 'good' your faith is based on the level of difficulty and if you keep your f***ing toes pointed and stuck the landing. Because the life of faith is a team sport, not an individual competition."

We're not in this battle alone. We're in it together. None of us has got it exactly right. We can't keep trying to hold everyone to our level of accountability. Certainly, not if we don't want them to hold us to theirs!

We can begin to make a difference—to truly bring justice to the misfits in our lives—when we can all find some common ground, shared space, to learn from one another. We must approach the Bible as a living, breathing document that helps us to understand our relationship with God and one another instead of a rule book etched in stone thousands of years ago. Then we can start to focus on what really matters: Loving one another the way God loves us.

THE IRONY OF GOD'S GRACE IS THAT ONCE WE RECEIVE IT, IT'S NO LONGER OURS TO HOLD.

Bonang Mohale, a great South African business leader, once said, "If we succeed and get it right, we will be lifting as we rise and learning from history because there is nothing more powerful as an exercise for the heart than extending a hand and lifting up another human being."

The irony of God's grace is that once we receive it, it's no longer ours to hold. We lift as we rise. As we come to truly understand God's love and acceptance in our own lives, we lift those who haven't been present to the same experience. As we rise on the tide of God's overflowing grace—even as misfits in our own unique ways—we are compelled to lift those still standing on the shore just waiting for someone to *be* God's love and grace to them.

Here's the thing, we might not have it all right. We probably don't. What if I'm wrong and God doesn't approve of women as ordained clergy leading, teaching, and preaching. What if I'm wrong? I'll take the risk.

If my mistake leads to even one more person experiencing the grace and love of God in a way they've never experienced before, that's a battle I'm willing to fight and a risk I'm willing to take.

Sometimes I find myself in doubt about the battles I feel God has put in my path. When I look around and see the crowd standing still, while someone else needs help, I try to remember Mama Merle. She didn't hesitate. She didn't wait for others to move. She stepped forward, took action, and showed the kind of love that goes beyond judgment and fear. And if anyone had questioned why she would bend to pick up a drunk man from the streets, I think she might have responded, "Blame it on Jesus."

This battle isn't a sprint. It might not even be a marathon. We probably won't see the full victory until we stand by Jesus. But the small victories along the way will be won with love. In the next chapter, we will look more closely about how Jesus teaches us to use love to overcome hate, so we can stay in this battle for the long haul.

Chapter 5
USE LOVE AS A WEAPON

I'VE KNOWN RANDY AUSTIN since we were kids. I'm a little bit older than him, but we won't talk about that. We met each other through music. Both of our families were in Gospel music so we often found ourselves at the same events. For a time, we sang together in a trio with our good friend Joseph Weaver.

As teenagers, I knew Randy was gay. Or at least I think I knew Randy was gay. Back in those days, it wasn't something we talked about. As I've said before, in the Gospel music world, the most common approach to most people's secrets was don't ask, don't tell.

At least I had an idea that Randy was gay. He was always the best dressed on the stage. I'll never forget one particular outfit. A red suit, with white, pearl buttons all the way down the front, a red shirt underneath and baggy, black pants. Hey, it was the 80s. I know that's stereotyping. But back then, that's what I understood it meant to be gay.

In any case, it never really mattered. I loved Randy. I never really considered his sexuality.

When Randy was in high school, he began to see that he didn't fit in. He grew up in a small North Texas town. He graduated with 24 other kids in his high school class. It's hard to lie low in a class that size.

Randy was an artistic kid. He'd much rather watch a Broadway show than a basketball game. Growing up in a small town, and graduating in a class of 25, he stuck out like a glittery, flamboyant thumb. He was bullied and ridiculed, and he took that to his tender heart. He describes much of his adolescence as living with a darkness that felt like a cloud around his head.

Randy grew up in a Christian home and was at church every time the doors opened. He didn't understand why God would have created him to feel so different from everyone else. He didn't understand why, as a creation of God, people wouldn't accept him for who he was.

The dark cloud—his depression—got so heavy that one night when he laid his head to sleep, he prayed to God.

"If you're real, God, and if you hear me praying right now, please show me that the way I feel is the way you created me to be. I can't go on like this if it's not," he prayed. "If you can't show me, I will end it all when I get up tomorrow."

Some people would call it a vision. Others would call it a dream. Randy calls it a life-changing moment where God showed up.

That night, as he slept, Randy saw himself walking down a gold path next to Jesus. He heard Jesus tell him that if God made all things perfect, then Randy was perfect too. When he woke, the cloud was gone. The darkness and shame that had covered his life for so long had lifted.

He got up that morning with the knowledge that God had a plan for his life that was bigger than anything he could plan for himself. He knew that God would use Randy's voice and his music and his songwriting to reach thousands of lives for God.

God fulfilled that promise as Randy's career in Christian music grew and his voice was heard in churches all over the country.

As he traveled, he heard preachers preach about Christ's love and acceptance even if he didn't always *experience* Christ's love and acceptance in those churches. His experience of love in church was one that came with conditions. He found enforcing the long list of rules was more important than showing grace and love to the people who broke them.

Like me in my early career, Randy knew the importance of keeping his life private. He knew his church friends would stay friends as long as they didn't ask and he didn't tell. So he continued singing and ministering to people while keeping his sexuality a secret.

Finally, he realized that his need to please the people in his life was overshadowing his desire to please God. He wasn't going to deny being a gay man anymore. He stopped hiding who he really was.

Randy's fears came true. The church rejected him. He was no longer welcome in the same churches where he had been leading people to God for years.

Randy was hurt. He was angry. But at the same time, he knew he was free from having to pretend to be someone he wasn't, and to try to live up to the expectations of people who didn't accept him for who he was. He knew God accepted him and that would be enough.

As life happens, over the years Randy and I went different directions and didn't see each other a lot. We stayed in touch with the occasional text or Facebook message. I watched him online as his music career evolved and he began touring all over the world with a country band. I listened to songs he wrote and released on his own. He was always a great singer, and I was so proud to see him continue to use his gifts.

Then, almost two years ago, Randy reached out to me and said he was going to visit our Crosswalk worship service for Easter. He'd been watching online and wanted to check it out. I had no idea how difficult that decision had been for Randy. I didn't know the rejection and hurt he had experienced during those years we didn't see each other.

As Randy tells it, his stomach was doing somersaults while he walked to the doors of our church that first Sunday. The memories of his experience in churches was threatening to overcome his desire to be in worship that morning.

But he said a little prayer and put one foot in front of the other.

The first person he met as he walked through the door was Veronica Knetig. To describe Veronica as one of our volunteers doesn't begin to explain the depth of commitment she has made to our church. She is our lead usher in Crosswalk, she serves with our mission teams, she does anything she's asked to do. She has been part of Crosswalk longer than me.

On this particular morning, Randy said when Veronica met him her face broke into a big smile, her arms opened wide and she welcomed him as she wrapped him in a hug. They had never met.

Veronica will tell you she's not a hugger. But God knew what Randy needed, and in that moment God used Veronica to provide it.

Randy knew he was in the right place. People continued to greet him and welcome him unconditionally as he entered the room. Standing at his seat, worshiping God as his true self that morning, he knew he was home.

That's how God uses love as a weapon to overcome hate.

Love is the Antidote

I get sick when I think of all the people who have been hurt by the church's misplaced judgment of people they don't understand. It brings tears to my eyes when I think of all the stories like Randy's I've heard over the years of people who have been rejected or literally kicked out of churches because they haven't lived up to their understanding or interpretation of righteousness.

Self-righteousness is more like it.

Love is the only antidote. I don't need to know your past to love you. I don't need to know if you're sober to love you. I don't need to know where you live to love you. And I don't need to know who you love to love you.

All I need to know is that God loves you. And I know that God loves you.

Love Our Way

We often think of love as an emotion. It's how we feel about someone or something. In its most basic form we define love in terms of the relationship between two people, especially romantic partners. The butterflies we get in our tummies when our favorite person walks in the room. Or the comfort our partner brings us in a difficult situation. Or the instinct that rises up in us when they need protection.

We also have love for our family members. Our parents. Our siblings. Our children. We have love for friends that have important places in our lives.

If we're *really* honest though, every love relationship we have is conditional. There are conditions to human love. We like to believe that our love is pure, but for that to be true, it would mean there is nothing another person could do that would cause us to remove our love.

When we are gaga in love with someone, we believe there's no way that relationship will end. Almost every relationship that turns into marriage or a long-term thing feels this way at the start. We can't even imagine being without that person.

Yet statistics tell us that almost half of all marriages end in divorce. Couples fall out of love. At some point, one or both of those partners discover the conditional aspects of their marriage. Maybe one cheats. Maybe their goals in life change. Maybe one just gets tired of picking up the other one's laundry! Whatever it is, their love is conditional.

Even marriages that survive the tests of time begin with conditions. Those conditions are even implied in the most standard wedding vows: "I take you to be my spouse for better, for worse, for richer, for poorer, in sickness and in health." Those vows seem all encompassing, but truthfully they imply the boundaries we set from the very beginning. When someone breaks the guidelines defined by those vows, the love is in danger of being lost.

As a relationship grows throughout the years, those boundaries become more defined. The partners learn what they expect from one another and those boundaries become part of what helps the relationship survive. We learn what to do to help our relationship grow. And we learn what not to do to keep it out of danger. Love isn't easy. It takes work.

Jeff and I went on our first date almost two years after my divorce. That divorce came shortly after my father passed away from a very brief illness and just before my mom, in her grief, moved with my brother, her sister, and her brother from Dallas to their hometown of Gulfport, Mississippi.

So, when Jeff and I met, I might have had some abandonment issues. We met at a moment, where I didn't trust that anything in my life would last.

At the same time, Jeff had never been married. He was in his 30s and never really been in a serious relationship. On our first date, he even told me, "I'm happy being alone. I don't see myself ever being married." I still love to remind him of that. We're lucky we even made it to the second date!

So, at our wedding one year and one month later, we still had some work to do. When we had disagreements, I wondered whether he would stay. Would he still want me? Would this be the thing that made him leave?

Jeff, a true introvert, had never shared his life with another person. Learning to be vulnerable and trust another person in his space—literally and figuratively—didn't always come easy for him.

But over time, we learned what our boundaries were and how to live within them. It takes work and it's not always easy. The work led to a trust that we can rely on one another. Even when we don't agree, we know we each have the other's best interest at heart. Shortly before we published this book, we celebrated our 20th anniversary and plan to live to see at least 20 more!

One of our best accomplishments is our son, Owen. He has grown to be a smart, kind, and intuitive young man. And he's funny. He can make us laugh. But nothing makes him laugh more than his dad. Though, Jeff usually says he's laughing *at* him and not *with* him. Maybe he's right!

The one human relationship we like to believe is unconditional is the love we have for our children. I can't imagine anything my son would do that could make me not love him. There are plenty of things he does that drive me crazy. There are plenty of things he did as a boy that required some sort of discipline. But I can't think of one thing that would make me not love him.

THE IRONY IS THAT WE SOMETIMES THINK REJECTION IS AN ACT OF LOVE.

Unfortunately not every parent can say that. I've met too many people in my ministry for whom the love of their parents was conditional. When their parents found out they were gay or identified as a different gender, they were cut out of their lives. When their parents found out they were dealing with drinking or using drugs, they kicked them out of the house. When the kid chose a path in life that didn't live up to their parents expectations, they wrote them off as failures.

That's using love as a weapon to hurt.

The irony is that we sometimes think rejection is an act of love. We say, "We still love them, but we can't condone their behavior. If we accept their behavior, they won't get better/change/get back on the right path." The religion-approved phrase is "Hate the sin. Love the sinner." This is a twisted understanding of love to virtually beat people into submission.

We want to justify our rejection as a response to a moral failure. The real moral failure comes in withholding our love from one another.

Redefining Love

Jesus redefines love for us. Jesus' love is unconditional. He extends his loving hand even to those who are marginalized, those who are considered unclean, sinners by the world's standards. He crosses ethnic, social and moral boundaries embodying a love that embraces the outcast.

In other words, his love doesn't look a whole lot like the way we define love today.

Jesus practices Agape love. This purest form of love is God's love for humanity. John 3:16 exemplifies Agape love: "For God so loved the world, that he gave his only Son, that whoever believes in him shall not perish, but have eternal life."

Christ's love is not an emotion, but an action that seeks the ultimate good of others.

Recently, I was talking about relationships with my good friend Justin Roark. The conversation started out of concern for mutual friends whose marriage was in trouble. It led to conversation about why some relationships seem to survive the test of time.

Justin said to me, "The only way a long-term relationship can last is when you put the other person first. In every decision you make, you consider your partner's needs above your own. Then, when they do the same for you, there's no way the relationship won't thrive."

Justin had just given the perfect explanation of Jesus' command to "love your neighbor as yourself." In many ways, that command sounds like an oxymoron. Jesus tells us to love our neighbor as ourselves because he knows we don't love anyone more than we love ourselves.

CHRIST'S LOVE IS NOT AN EMOTION, BUT AN ACTION THAT SEEKS THE ULTIMATE GOOD OF OTHERS.

Me. I'm number one. It's human nature. It's survival of the fittest. We have evolved to believe that the only way to survive is to put ourselves first. It creates a paradox, as if instincts for self-preservation and the altruistic impulses of love might be at odds.

If we love ourselves the most, how can we love our neighbor the same?

That's the miracle of Christ's love.

The miracle of Christ's love leads us to put others before ourselves. When we can truly accept the sacrificial love that Christ gave to us—that Agape love—we can't help but respond in the same way.

Sacrificially.

Putting others before ourselves. That means loving all people the way we love ourselves—as if they are the most important people in the world.

That's not always easy to do. In fact, it's really hard. Not everyone is lovable. But if we want to fight hate, it starts with love.

The only antidote to hate is love.

Until the world is filled with more love than hate, it will always be a battle. What that's you say? That sounds like an impossible task? You might be right! But, I believe that nothing is impossible with the love of God on our side.

Love can overcome hate. Love will overcome hate. Love does overcome hate.

Changing Our Hearts

Changing the world sounds like a big job. So, where do we start? We start with our own hearts. We start by examining our own motivations. Our own prejudices. Our own misunderstandings of what it means to love.

Where do you have hate in your heart? I know, you're thinking, "But DeDe, I don't hate anyone!" You need to look deeper. We all have prejudice baked into us from our upbringing, from our community, from our experiences. That's the same thing as hate. Examine those things. Understand why you feel the way you do. Work on forgiving the person, the situation, the community that led you to those feelings.

Love often requires forgiveness. For many people, hate is bred from abuse, perceived injustice, and other people's poor decisions. We can't love again until we deal with the cause of our hate.

Every week, we have more and more people like Randy who walk through our church doors. They've been hurt by the church. More specifically, they've been hurt by people in the church. Their response could be to develop a hate for the church. For some, the result is to fester a hate for God.

I can't begin to tell you about the heartbreaking conversations I've had with people about their experiences in church. Stories of abuse. Stories of rejection. Stories of deception. All in the name of Jesus!

I won't lie. In these conversations, I understand what it means to hate. It's difficult to find compassion or forgiveness for these church folk who have twisted God's word to reject God's children.

But like the people I meet, I have to fight that hate with love. I have to remember that they too are children of God who have been shaped by misinterpreted theology and hurtful communities. So I pray for them. I pray that they will experience God's love in the same way I have. As unconditional. As unlimited. As eternally available.

Just Show Up

In the midst of a hurting, conflicted world, often fighting hate is to just show up. Just. Show. Up. Be present to other hurting people. Show them what it means to love them the way you love yourself. Let them see God's love shine through you.

And be prepared to be hurt again. Jesus told us to love other people as ourselves. He didn't say they'd always love us back. He never promised us easy. When we start to open our hearts to people who have been hurt, rejected and abused, we have to expect to be hurt. We may be the first person who showed them that kind of love. They may not trust our love to be authentic.

Often fighting hate is to just show up. Just. Show. Up.

They may not trust the love they feel rising in their own hearts to be authentic. People are comfortable in their own "uncomfortableness." So when we start to feel comfortable, we don't know what to do with it. We want to find the way back to our discomfort.

You know people like that. You may be a person like that. It's easier to complain than to be happy! I don't know why that is, but human beings love to complain. I live in Texas. It's hotter than hell in Texas. One hot summer day, I saw a sign hanging in a store. It said, "I miss complaining about it being cold outside." In Texas, we complain so much when it's hot that we start to miss complaining when it's cold. There's always something to complain about!

So, when we start to love people without conditions, they are going to get uncomfortable. They may not know what to do with our love. And they may reject it in the process.

When that happens, here's what you know. You know you did what Christ called you to do. You're going to release that person back into the harsh world. You're going to pray that the love you showed them caused a chink in their defensive armor and that they will experience that same love from someone else who will finally break through.

Then, you're going to pick yourself up, dust off your wounded pride, and show up for the next person you meet. Because that's what God called you to do. That's what Christ did for you.

Jesus the Misfit

Jesus doesn't just gather with the misfits of his time—the people other religious people think are unworthy, unclean, or unrighteous—he *is* a misfit of his time too. He stands in opposition to the social and religious norms of the day, making him a misfit of the society where he lives. He stands out because his teachings and actions to love even the misfits clash with religious and cultural expectations.

The Lost.

He can associate with social outcasts because he knows what it's like to be one. Jesus dines with tax collectors, a scandalous act to the religious leaders of the time. Tax collectors are often seen as traitors and corrupt because of their role in collecting taxes for the Roman authorities. But Jesus' visit to the home of Zacchaeus, the chief tax collector in Jericho, leads to Zacchaeus' repentance and restitution (Luke 19:1-10). In spite of the persecution he will receive from the Pharisees, Jesus focuses on his mission to love the lost.

The Outcast.

Jesus also reaches out to lepers. According to Jewish law, lepers are unclean and sent to live in isolation away from the rest of society. By touching and healing lepers, Jesus shows us his willingness to break social stigmas and show love to the outcasts of society (Mark 1:40-45). While religious elites see these acts as nasty and vile, the acts themselves underscore the inclusivity of Jesus' ministry.

The Sick.

One time Jesus and his disciples got out of their boat in an area called Gerasenes. This is a Gentile community where most Jewish rabbis will not visit. Yet, Jesus travels there and performs one of his most dramatic miracles—the exorcism of the Gerasene man possessed by a legion of demons (Mark 5:1-20). Jesus loves the man enough to heal him by sending the demons into a herd of pigs that run off the cliff and drown.

Jesus knows what it means to love a misfit, because he is one.

His teachings on love and forgiveness are radical in his time. Teaching to love one's enemies and to turn the other cheek contradicts the "eye for an eye" teaching of the Old Testament. He just doesn't fit in with the other religious teachers.

Even the concept of the Kingdom of God, as Jesus preaches, is revolutionary. He speaks of a kingdom, not of this world, but one that upends the importance of wealth and power, and values the lowly and meek. The Kingdom of God is filled with misfits!

We can't truly begin to fight hate with love until we recognize ourselves as misfits too. We can't overcome hate by holding ourselves above others as if we have the unique solution to their problems. We can only overcome hate when we acknowledge that we are broken, damaged and injured people who need love as equally as everyone else.

Randy has hardly missed a Sunday since that Easter morning he first walked into Crosswalk. He has found his place in our merry band of misfits! He's now singing with us every Sunday and serving as our music producer for Lovers Lane Worship.

He has been a game changer for our ministry. He knows the message of Christ's Agape love is one the world needs to hear because he has experienced it. Through Randy's leadership we created Lovers Lane Worship, and we have begun to write and record music with a message of love and acceptance with our band leader and chosen little brother, Rafe Grigar. Randy doesn't know it, but we wouldn't even be writing this book if God hadn't brought him back into our lives.

We can never underestimate the power of God's love to change the world—one life at a time. Randy walked through our doors and as a result we are reaching even more misfits around the globe through our music and this book than we ever have before.

When love overcomes hate, a community of people who don't all look alike, think alike, act alike begins to grow. We become a community that values one another for our status as children of God and not by our politics, our pasts, or our potential. We become a community that becomes filled with better individuals because we learn from the different viewpoints, experiences and lifestyles of people who aren't exactly like us. Our individual lives become enriched and in turn, the world becomes a better place. When people ask us, how can you love *those* people, we can just say, "Blame it on Jesus."

In a world that is becoming more and more polarized, loving ALL people is a countercultural idea. So, how do we have the confidence to live more counterculturally like Jesus? We'll talk more about that in the next chapter.

Chapter 6
SHAKE THINGS UP

T HROUGHOUT THE YEARS I'VE served in various churches, special people have joined me along my journey. We've created great friendships together as we have supported one another through the ups and downs of life.

We call this group "Real Hope", and we meet a couple of times a month for Bible study. We serve together in mission projects that focus on homelessness and hunger. And we do an annual Christmas concert to raise money for homeless ministries in Dallas.

One of our regular projects has been to deliver basic essentials to people living on the streets. We start by gathering together and assembling bags of toothpaste, tooth brushes, toilet paper, socks, t-shirts, bottled water, and other basic necessities. Then we head downtown and find the local gathering spots and pass out the bags along with bottles of water.

It can be a heart-wrenching experience walking through these tent communities that pop up around town. We are fully aware that homelessness is another hot political topic. People might say that when we hand out these bags, we are encouraging people to live on the street. We know that it may be less efficient and effective compared to the larger programs and organizations. In fact, as a group we also wholeheartedly support those organizations with our gifts of money and time.

But we believe this kind of support helps provide a balanced approach to the long-term solutions of these established groups by offering a small amount of relief to the immediate needs of people in need. Plus, I believe this is what Jesus would have done. He would push back against the cultural expectations and go to meet the people where they are.

One weekend, we were handing out bags near one of the local homeless shelters. At this particular shelter, people were able to sleep there at night, but they had to leave during the day. So, many of them gathered outside the shelter throughout the day until they were let back in that afternoon.

When we arrived, we split into small groups to pass out supplies. It was a hot day and the bottled water was popular. The sun was shining without a cloud in the sky. A community had gathered in groups on the sidewalks and a couple of open lots near the shelter. A few people had set up tents or strung up tarps to protect themselves from the heat. Others huddled under any patch of shade they could find. A few trees. Near the edge of a building. Even the long narrow shadow created by a telephone pole.

The people looked like you would expect a group of people who lived on the streets to look. Most of them were by themselves. There were a few children. Even in the heat, many of them wore several layers because it was all the clothing they owned. What few belongings they had were gathered into whatever type of bag they might have been able to find, save, or collect. Plastic grocery bags. Paper grocery bags. Old gym bags. Suitcases.

The people looked tired. They were tired. Living without a home is exhausting. A lot more exhausting than having a job and a clean, cool place to live. The idea that people live this way because it's easier than working is crazy to me.

The only people who could say that haven't actually met these people. It's a lot easier to villainize people you haven't met.

As we continued winding our way throughout the gathered community, I heard a woman's voice calling from behind me. "Hey lady. Hey purple hair. Hey lady."

The voice was getting louder and as I turned, I saw a woman heading in my direction. She had this unruly, patch of orange hair on her head. Her pants were bright red and she was wearing a t-shirt with a cartoon character on the front. She wasn't carrying anything, so she must have left her belongings sitting nearby somewhere.

I could feel the men in my little group tense up and go into defense mode as this woman leaned forward and continued to charge toward me, pointing and calling, "Hey lady. Hey purple hair." But I saw her eyes wide open with joy and her face lit up with the most beautiful smile. I knew we were safe.

She stopped hard just short of running into me and said, "You're that lady that sings, right? I heard you sing at that church."

When I asked what church, she said, "I came on a bus. You sang at that church."

It had been at least two years since I'd sung at Citchurch. In many ways, that broke my heart knowing this woman had been living on the streets this whole time. In other ways, it warmed my heart to know that the ministry at Citichurch had created some kind of good memory for her.

She told me her name was Silvia and said, "Would you sing a song for me?"

"I will if you sing with me?" I responded. "How about Amazing Grace?"

"Oh I love Amazing Grace," she said with a smile.

And so we sang together. In an empty lot surrounded by a gathering of people who the world would consider misfits.

I felt Jesus' presence there in that moment with Silvia more than I'd ever felt singing with the most talented musicians in a giant church surrounded by people the world would consider righteous.

A Countercultural Jesus

Living like Jesus means living counter culturally. It means going against the grain of what society expects of us. Because too often, society gets it wrong. In fact, too often our fellow Christians get it wrong. In our effort to emphasize "doctrinal purity," moral boundaries, and a prophetic stance against modern society, our approach can be more judgmental than loving.

Even though we claim to be countercultural like Jesus, we often end up in an "us vs. them" battle that keeps us from being open and inclusive to them—one of the most important themes of Jesus' ministry. Jesus didn't identify with just one group. Jesus broke down the boundaries of the day and reached out to everyone.

Christians today often see ourselves as under attack by modern culture, and we go into defense mode. Putting up walls and getting defensive. That's not what Jesus does. He builds open, honest relationships. When he is challenged, he doesn't retreat and hide from the world. He engages deeply with the people in it, even those who are morally questionable by the standards of the day.

When we talk about judgment versus compassion, it's clear where Jesus stands. He isn't afraid to call out what is wrong, but he always follows up with empathy, compassion, and love. He understands the spirit of the law rather than nitpicking the letter of the law.

Sometimes, in an effort to protect what's seen as moral and correct, there's a risk that Christians prioritize moral and cultural superiority. When we do, we stifle the empathy and understanding that are central to a Christ-like love.

Love Over Fear

Fear of losing traditional values or being overwhelmed by societal changes can lead us to try and tighten our grip on the world around us in an effort to control it. But the Bible reminds us that perfect love drives out fear (1 John 4:18).

Look, I know people don't want homeless camps on the end of their perfect, safe, neighborhoods. I'm no saint. That's not what I want either. But much of our approach to homelessness is driven by fear. Fear of the unknown, fear of those who are different, and fear of how homelessness reflects us as a society. This leads to avoidance, judgment, or even retribution. These fears can prevent us from truly addressing the problem with empathy, compassion, and love.

Jesus reminds us that our approach to any challenge we face should be rooted in love, not fear. Perfect love moves us toward understanding, action, and care. Instead of focusing on the discomfort or risks, Jesus challenges us to view the homeless and other issues with dignity, compassion, and the desire to help, not punish. It calls us to see people's humanity rather than their circumstances and to respond to them with practical, loving action.

As it relates to homelessness, this means advocating for policies and community efforts that prioritize compassionate solutions—such as shelter, mental health care, job opportunities, and outreach programs—over responses that punish. When we approach homelessness with love, we become part of creating solutions that heal rather than hurt.

Stepping In, Not Out

Jesus modeled a love that embraced changes and challenges, always trusting in God's overarching plan instead of succumbing to fear. This kind of love involves a lot of trust and a willingness to step into the unknown, confident that God's purposes will prevail, even if the journey is unpredictable. But that's what faith is!

Fear can lead to isolation. If we define countercultural as pulling away from society, we have taken a step in the wrong direction. Jesus steps into society, not away. He uses everyday situations and cultural contexts familiar to his audience to share his teachings. His parables and lessons are grounded in the everyday lives of the people he spoke to, making his teachings relevant and understandable.

Stepping back into a protective cultural shell leads to isolation, and moves away from Jesus' example of being deeply involved in the world, actively participating in it, and living out the values that often challenged the status quo.

It's crucial for us as Christian to continually check ourselves to see if our countercultural label is actually helping us live out Jesus' teachings of love and grace. Or are we building walls that keep us from fulfilling the Gospel's call to love the misfits—our neighbors, strangers, and even enemies effectively? Are we truly following Jesus' example, breaking down barriers and spreading love and understanding in a world that desperately needs it?

As our culture's understanding of homosexuality becomes more clear, open and accepting, it threatens many of the traditionally held views of modern Christianity. For those who fear the changes this might bring, they take on the countercultural banner by further restricting their biblical understanding of homosexuality and using it to exclude and reject people in the LGBTQ+ community from their place in the church.

Some even use their pulpits to encourage our government to withhold basic rights from gay people. They see themselves as fighting the culture that threatens their faith, when actually they are building walls that prevent them from living into Christ's message of love and grace.

Living out a Christ-like countercultural love means venturing into challenging and sometimes uncomfortable places. It means showing love and grace in situations where it's not the easiest or most convenient option. It's about making choices that reflect self-sacrifice, not self-interest. That's what Jesus does.

Jesus the Disrupter

Jesus doesn't stop at challenging social norms. He frequently butts heads with the religious bigwigs of his time, like the Pharisees and Sadducees. He calls them out for being "whitewashed tombs"—pretty on the outside but dead on the inside (Matthew 23:27-28). He stresses the importance of the spirit of the law over the letter of the law, emphasizing genuine faith, mercy, and justice rather than just going through the motions of empty rituals and maintaining appearances.

Forgiveness. Jesus' teachings center on love and forgiveness. In the Sermon on the Mount (Matthew 5:38-44), he tells his followers to love their enemies and pray for those who persecute them, which is a total change from the eye-for-an-eye mentality of the time. His message promotes a radical kind of love and forgiveness aimed at reconciliation and peace, rather than revenge and hostility.

Women. Jesus also makes waves in how he treats women. In a time when women are often seen and not heard, Jesus speaks directly to them, teaches them, and values their company. We see it in his interactions with the Samaritan woman at the well, Mary Magdalene, and Mary and Martha (John 4:7-26).

This is groundbreaking in a patriarchal society where women are often considered property. In those days, it's not unusual for a father to make a deal with the farmer down the road that includes a cow, two pigs, some chickens and, oh "my daughter to be your wife." Jesus' countercultural actions and teachings affirm the value and spiritual equality of women, treating them with respect and dignity that is often not afforded to them.

Simplicity. Rejecting materialism and status is another cornerstone of Jesus' teaching. He leads a simple life and warns about the dangers of wealth, urging people to prioritize spiritual richness over accumulating material wealth (Matthew 6:19-21). His teachings challenge the cultural equating of wealth and status with success and divine favor, highlighting the importance of relying on God rather than earthly possessions. Look out prosperity gospel!

Peace. Even his stand on violence sets him apart. In an era marked by Roman occupation and frequent uprisings, Jesus advocates for peace and nonviolence. When Peter draws his sword to protect him, Jesus rebukes him and reminds him that "those who live by the sword will die by the sword" (Matthew 26:52). His commitment to nonviolence and loving enemies stands in contrast to the prevailing attitudes of resistance and retaliation.

Jesus doesn't just challenge the norms of his time. He sets a transformative example for us as his followers. He calls us to live out principles of love, justice, mercy, and humility, which are revolutionary then and continue to challenge us today. His life encourages us to look beyond societal norms and live in ways that reflect deeper truths and values.

That day when I was standing on the street singing "Amazing Grace" with Sylvia, I remembered one of my favorite stories about Jesus in the Bible.

The Gospels of Matthew, Mark, and Luke all tell the story of a woman who has been dealing with a health issue for about twelve years—she is constantly bleeding, which, according to the laws back then, makes her ritually unclean. This means she can't touch people or things because she will make them unclean too. You can imagine how isolating and lonely life is for her, being cut off from society with a feeling of overwhelming hopelessness.

One day, she hears that Jesus is in town and she sets out to find him. I imagine it is a hot day, with no clouds in the sky. She may have tried to find a small patch of shade against a wall or under a tree to wait for Jesus to pass by.

She has heard all about the miracles he's been performing, and she thinks to herself, "If I can just touch even his clothes, I'll be healed." She waits and finally, Jesus arrives. Despite the crowds around him, she is able to sneak up behind him and to just touch the edge of his cloak.

Immediately, she feels the change in her body—she is healed just like that! But Jesus notices something too. He feels the power go out of him, so he turns around in the crowd and asks, "Who touched my clothes?" His disciples say, "Look at this crowd, everyone's pushing against you, and you're asking who touched you?" But Jesus keeps looking to see who has touched him.

The woman realizes she can't stay hidden, so she comes forward, trembling with fear. She falls down in front of him and tells him the truth about what she has done and why. And here's the beautiful part: Jesus doesn't scold her. He speaks to her with love. He says, "Daughter, your faith has healed you. Go in peace and be free from your suffering."

Despite the strict rules of his time, Jesus doesn't shun the woman when she reaches out to touch the hem of his garment. Instead, he responds with empathy, compassion, and love breaking all the social and religious taboos in the process.

Jesus' interaction with her goes beyond just a miraculous healing. He publicly acknowledges her, calling her "daughter" and commending her faith, which not only heals her physically, but also restores her dignity and status in the community. This recognition is groundbreaking and disruptive.

By praising her faith in front of a crowd that would have been surprised or even uncomfortable with her impurity and boldness, Jesus challenges everyone there to rethink their own prejudices and expectations about worth and purity. He teaches that faith and a personal connection with God are far more important than blindly following ritualistic laws.

There was a man named Julio Diaz. He was a social worker in New York City. One evening, Julio Diaz ended his subway commute one stop early, as usual, to eat at his favorite diner. However, this night was different. As he stepped off the train, a teenage boy approached him and pulled out a knife, demanding his wallet. Diaz complied without hesitation, handing over his wallet.

But as the robber began to walk away, Diaz called out to him, offering his coat as well. Startled, the teenager turned back, puzzled. Diaz then told him that he was heading to dinner and invited the young man to join him.

Surprisingly, the teenager accepted. They went to the diner together, where Diaz regularly dined. The staff greeted him warmly, and the teenager noticed this community respect. As they ate, they talked about life, choices, and consequences. Diaz gently pressed the young man about his life choices and what he truly wanted out of life, beyond the immediate desperation that had driven him to robbery.

When the bill came, Diaz told the teenager that he'd have to get the check because, after all, he still had Diaz's wallet. The young man handed the wallet back without a word. Diaz paid for the meal and gave the boy 20 dollars, asking only that he hand over the knife, which the teenager did before leaving.

Julio Diaz's response to a threatening situation by extending kindness and an invitation to conversation rather than reacting with fear or aggression turned a potential violent encounter into a life lesson for both. Diaz later said that his approach was rooted in a belief that treating people with dignity and kindness has the power to transform behavior more effectively than reactive punishment.

Changing the world starts with one act of love and compassion. It almost never starts with political action or legal challenges or sweeping social reform. It starts with an individual act of love.

Jesus is our example.

Justifying Justice

The world is changing. Our culture is changing. While gay people, divorced people, addicts, brown people, immigrants, women, homeless people have been marginalized by society, they are starting to find more acceptance and their rightful place in the world. It's not perfect, and there's still a long way to go, but change has started to happen.

In ways I don't understand, many people of faith feel threatened by this change. Instead of being a part of the solution, they use scripture to actively try to impede this progress.

If we're using scripture to justify hate toward other people, we're doing something wrong. Oh people will say, "We don't hate them" or "We're trying to help them" or "We're just showing them tough love." They'll pull out the tired old "Hate the sin, love the sinner" excuse.

But I've met the people they're giving tough love to—I've been the person on the receiving end of that tough love. It looks and feels a whole lot like hate to me.

When we use scripture to justify our injustice, we conveniently ignore other passages that might get in our way. Too often, we find value in a fixed interpretation of scripture arguing that its divine origin, clarity, history, and role in providing moral and cultural stability have set its meaning in stone. The fear for some is that taking a fresh look at scripture will somehow dilute its meaning or mitigate its power.

Jesus, on the other hand, uses established scripture to justify justice. He has a knack for taking a fresh look at traditional scripture, digging deeper into its meaning and how it has been applied to the people around him. He isn't concerned with changing the law, but about intensifying its relevance, without diluting its power.

When Jesus goes to eat with Matthew, the Pharisees question the disciples, asking, "Why does your teacher eat with tax collectors and sinners?" Jesus hears this and responds "Healthy people don't need a doctor, but sick people do. Go and learn what this means: I want mercy and not sacrifice. I didn't come to call righteous people, but sinners" (Matthew 9:12-13).

Jesus is quoting Hosea 6:6 from the Old Testament, where God expresses his preference for mercy over sacrifice. He redefines the scripture to mean that the heart's attitude in worship is more important than mere outward religious observances. Jesus uses this scripture to justify his engagement with those who others consider unrighteous and unworthy. He challenges the Pharisees to reconsider their understanding of what God truly values—acts of kindness, love, and mercy more than ritualistic adherence to rules.

During his Sermon on the Mount, Jesus doesn't just repeat the Old Testament commandment against murder. He expands it to show that even unjustified anger and insults can be morally equivalent to murder. He doesn't just reinterpret the law for the times. He urges people to understand the true spirit of the law—encouraging an internal vigilance that goes beyond simply avoiding physical acts of violence. He highlights a deeper moral principle that underlies the literal text. Ethical principles aren't confined to specific cultural or legal contexts, but are universal.

Jesus justifies justice with the same scripture the other religious leaders of the time use to hurt people.

Another time, Jesus gets into it with the Pharisees about their rigid observance of the Sabbath. The Pharisees catch his disciples picking some grain to eat on the Sabbath, which is a big no-no in their books. But Jesus fires back, reminding them of a story about David, who once did something similar when he and his friends are hungry.

Jesus isn't just being argumentative. He is showing that the law's intention isn't to impose hardship, but to ensure welfare and mercy. His punchline, "I desire mercy, not sacrifice," drives the point home—God wants compassion and understanding, not blind adherence to rules.

Far from weakening the law's power, Jesus' interpretations enrich its meaning, making it more dynamic and applicable to everyday life. His countercultural way of reading and applying scripture shakes up the status quo and encourages a more profound moral engagement, one that considers both the letter and the spirit of the law.

It is wrong to make anyone feel hated, left out, marginalized, ostracized, or minimized—especially in the name of Jesus. That's not what Jesus says to do. I'll say it again. That's not what Jesus says to do.

Lead with Love

When the legal expert asks Jesus what the most important commandment is, he says, "Love the Lord your God" and secondly, "Love your neighbor as yourself" (Matthew 22:36-40).

It's unfortunate that it might be considered countercultural to encourage us to love one another, but there are too many people who continue to be pushed to the side by Christians. A few years ago, I would have said the misfits of the world have been forgotten by people of faith. But today, some people have remembered the misfits, and are actively working to remove their basic human rights, to reverse their gains, and to further push them down.

WHEN WE USE OUR INDIVIDUAL VOICES FOR LOVE,
WE CAN COME TOGETHER AS A CHORUS OF CHANGE.

All too often it is our Christian brothers and sisters who are leading this charge.

It's time for the rest of us to shake things up and to lead with love. Always lead with love. When we use our individual voices for love, we can come together as a chorus of change.

When we seek to truly live a life like Jesus, we will live a way that changes our world. Because the way Jesus lives is counter to the way much of our world works right now.

Jesus eats with the outcasts. He stands up for the marginalized. He prays for his enemies. He gives voice to the voiceless. He calls out the hypocrites.

Our church, Lovers Lane United Methodist Church, has begun working with a ministry in Brownsville, Texas, a town caught in the midst of the border crisis in our country. We send a team of volunteers to serve with a wonderful ministry called Team Brownsville whose goal is to help families and individuals legally seeking asylum in the United States. Our team helps serve meals to those waiting on both sides of the border.

Immigration is another hot-button topic in our world today. It's a complicated issue. There are economic implications, cultural changes, and questions of legal and moral responsibilities to people seeking asylum in the United States. I don't think it's a coincidence that these people are often referred to as "aliens," literally classifying them as misfits.

Jesus would probably remind us that whichever side of the political issue we fall, we should always remember that these misfits are first and foremost children of God. Lead with love.

When our team returns from their trips, they don't come back and report on the political complexities of immigration. They return with stories of people they meet who are hungry and who they are able to feed.

They return with stories of people who are filled with gratitude because they have been treated with dignity in an undignified situation. They tell stories of people who find a glimmer of hope, even if only for a moment.

It's a lot easier to hate people you haven't met. It's a lot easier to love people who you have met.

Here's the thing, it's not always easy to live like Jesus. We've talked about that a lot in this book. When you take a stand against the things that society considers "normal" you're going to meet resistance. When you take a stand that some of your fellow Christians consider "normal," well Katie bar the door. They will come after you. They will try to paint you as unChristian, immoral, and sinful.

Their language will be hateful and divisive. But you are standing on the shoulders of the man who defines what it means to go against the culture of the day by fighting hate with love. So when you start to shake things up and people tell you you're wrong, you tell them to take it to the cross and "Blame it on Jesus."

So what does it mean to take it to the cross? In the next chapter, we will talk about how taking our worries, burdens, and fears to the cross can free us to rely on Jesus.

Chapter 7
TAKE IT TO THE CROSS

B OB BAKER HAS GAINED several nicknames over the 20 years we've been friends. "Bobaker" because when my son was young, he always referred to Bob by his full name in a way that sounded like one, long word. "B-I-L" because as the husband to Brenda Baker, my best friend and chosen sister, he's also my chosen Brother-in-Law. But "Trouble" is probably my favorite name for him. I think it speaks for itself!

I met Bob when I applied for my first full-time church job after winding down my time as a touring singer. I'd felt the call to be in church ministry for a few years but had resisted it. I'd spent a lot of time in churches, so I knew church people. We church people aren't always easy. My first encounter with Bob made me start to think I might have been right to wait so long.

Following several phone conversations and one in-person meeting with the church's senior pastor, Ken Diehm, we scheduled a meeting with the search committee for a group interview. When I walked in, it felt a little more like a firing line.

There were at least 20 people on this committee, and Bob was one of them. Their questions revealed their passion for the music ministry at this church. They had a strong program for several years, but faced some challenges more recently. I could feel the hurt in their questions.

I only remember one question that day and it came from Bob.

He asked, in a frank tone that seemed to challenge my ability, "Over the past few years, the number of people in our choir has declined. What would you do to get more people to join us?"

I looked directly at Bob and said, "Well, we will make this the best choir this church has ever seen. When people hear *this* choir, they will be asking to join us. We won't have to ask them."

Bob sat back, folded his arms and smiled.

After the interview, Bob greeted me warmly, shook my hand and said, "I hope we weren't too hard on you."

I responded with a smile, "Not at all. But I can tell you're going to be trouble."

God Knows

Though Bob grew up in a Christian home, he left his faith behind as a young man. He had lost a brother to illness at an early age. His relationship with his father was fraught with challenges. He has said he just didn't see the need for God. For much of his life he considered himself agnostic.

Even so, Bob has always been a good man. He recently retired and at his retirement party, I was struck by the stories I heard from people who'd known Bob for many, many years, even before he became a Christian. They revealed Bob to be a kind and caring man, always ready to lend a helping hand.

I could see that even though Bob didn't know God back then, God always knew Bob.

Bob met Brenda in 1985. Unlike Bob, Brenda grew up in the Nazarene church and had a deep faith her whole life. You will not meet a more loving human being than Brenda Baker. Through Brenda's love, Bob became a Christian.

If you asked Bob if he had any regrets about his time before finding his faith, it might be that he wasn't always able to be as present for his children as he would have liked. He has always had a relationship with his children and has worked to make it as strong as it can be. But as so often happens in divorce, separation from their mother also created some separation between him and his kids.

Bob and Brenda have been in ministry with me since we first met. After several years at that first church, they joined me on my journey from church to church until finally finding our place at Lovers Lane United Methodist Church in Dallas where we are now. In many ways, they are partners in ministry with me and Jeff. We can count on them to help in any way needed.

Before Crosswalk, when I first started singing at Citichurch, the church filled with half LGBTQ+ people and half homeless people, Bob and Brenda were with me on my first Sunday. Bob fully admits that he was hesitant about being in a church filled with gay people. He hadn't known many gay people at that time. When they arrived, Bob sat next to Mike and Jake, two men who were clearly in a relationship together. They greeted Bob and Brenda warmly and welcomed them to their church.

Over the months we were at Citichurch, Mike and Jake became important people in Bob's life. And Bob became an important person in theirs. Even though Mike and Jake's relationship ended, Bob and Brenda have stayed in touch with each of them ever since.

Now, Bob has become the father figure of our Crosswalk worship community. Every Sunday morning, before and after worship, he moves through the room greeting as many people as he can. He makes a special effort to meet and welcome anyone he doesn't recognize.

Many of the people in Crosswalk don't have relationships with their own parents. They've been rejected because of their sexuality or because of their addictions or because of some past choices they've made in their life.

Bob helps bridge that gap. A straight, white, man who literally opens his arms to them without questions.

God has used Bob throughout his life, even when Bob didn't know it.

Bob connects with people who doubt their own faith, because he has doubted his. Bob becomes a stand-in father and grandfather, because his life has shown him the importance of those roles in life. Bob makes the misfits feel welcome, because he has taken the time to get to know and love other people just like them.

Bob's not perfect. I haven't stopped calling him Trouble! But God's not waiting for any of us to be perfect to be of good use. Even as we work to become better people, God will use us—our doubts, our flaws, our mistakes, our past and our gifts—to shine God's light into people's dark places.

Perfection Not Required

As we take on this challenge to fight hate with love and to stand up for the misfits around us, we doubt our ability to be the voice of change. We doubt our right to be heard. We doubt our authority to be that chance for someone else. We doubt our worthiness.

> GOD'S NOT WAITING FOR ANY OF US TO BE PERFECT TO BE OF GOOD USE.

Even when we know we don't have to be perfect to receive God's love and we preach, talk, pray, support, cheer on, and yell "Amen" to the idea that ALL people are not just tolerated by God but fully loved by God, we can often harbor a small (or maybe big) doubt in our own minds that we are worthy of that group.

The world is full of misfits. And yes, you are one too. I am one, too. We all have some issues to contend with. I was joking with some friends recently that we can't trust anyone who claims to have no issues.

When we boast about our perfections, we run the risk of coming off as self-righteous. If we want to make a difference in the world, we must be honest about our shortcomings. Honest with ourselves and with other people. We have to be vulnerable and approachable. We can't identify with the hurting souls around us when we can't relate to their pain. And if we've got it all figured out, we might as well lay down and die right now. What's the point of life if we're not constantly moving forward?

Donna and Dolly

One of my mentors in life is Rev. Donna Whitehead. Donna is a retired pastor still serving in ministry at Lovers Lane. I don't think she would mind me telling you that she is well into her 70s.

Donna has a fantastic story. She comes from a humble background in a small town in northern Louisiana. She raised a family while going to seminary at a time when most women were still staying at home. She became one of the first women ordained in the United Methodist Church. You should read her book, *I Am Enough: A memoir for spiritual seekers*. You will be inspired by her story.

I've learned so much from Donna over the years I've known her. She always lends an ear and gives sound advice when I'm having trouble. She has more energy on her worst day than I do on my best. What she has taught me most is that it's never too late to learn something new.

Donna knows that I love me some Dolly Parton. Not only do I love Dolly's music, but I love her approach to life. She lives with joy, and she has a message of love and full acceptance of everyone.

Over the past few years, Donna has also become a fan of Dolly Parton. In true Donna fashion, she wanted to learn all she could about Dolly and asked me if I would go to Dollywood with her! So, that's what we did. One Sunday after church, we got in our car and drove to Pigeon Forge, Tennessee, with stops along the way in Memphis and Nashville. Every mile we drove was an opportunity for Donna to learn something new. We stayed in a small condo in Pigeon Forge, ate great southern food, and soaked in all things Dolly.

Donna's fascination with Dolly isn't just about her music, her costumes, her hair, or anything else that gets Dolly attention—though those things are all great! It's really about her approach to life. It's about her joy and the message of love and acceptance she brings to the world.

Donna is passionate about evangelism, and she knows Dolly is the ultimate evangelist. Dolly has a way of making people feel welcome and loved, and she doesn't limit her acceptance to the rich and famous. She stands for the misfits of life and, in fact, proudly counts herself among them. Dolly has something to teach us all.

One of the reasons Donna is so successful at helping churches grow is that she, like Dolly, is genuinely interested in every person she meets.

When you meet Donna, be prepared for the questions. She wants to know you and learn from you.

In any conversation I have with her, she doesn't just dole out advice and wisdom—though she has plenty to provide. Conversations with her are a two-way street. She listens as much as she talks because she wants to know what you think.

Donna—and Dolly, for that matter—know they don't have it all figured out. They might not even get it all right. But they are both always trying to be better.

Living by Grace

Paul's letter to the Ephesians teaches us that we don't need to have our lives perfectly lined up to start living out our faith. Right from the beginning of his letter, Paul makes it clear that grace and salvation are gifts from God. We get them through faith, not because we've earned them with good deeds or flawless behavior. It's about what God does, not what we do. Anyone can start right where they are, mess and all.

Paul writes about how the Jews and Gentiles, who have diverse and sometimes conflicting backgrounds, come together under one faith through Jesus. This unity doesn't require that anyone be perfect to join. It invites them to grow together and to learn from each other's differences.

Paul says that maturing in faith is a journey. The church should be here to help everyone, no matter where they are on this path, to understand

Jesus and to grow closer to God's hopes for them. Our faith journey is an ongoing, step-by-step process of shedding our old selves and embracing a new life shaped by God's grace.

Paul's letter to the Ephesians is an open invitation to jump into faith feet first, no matter our past or present state. It's a reassuring message that the Christian faith is inclusive, meant for growth and transformation, and everyone is welcome to start their journey at any point.

Jesus welcomes us to the table, knowing we have more to learn but also that our life experience, accumulated knowledge, and willingness to fulfill his mission make us worthy of his call. Jesus invites us to join all the other misfits at the table so we can learn what it really means to be loved unconditionally. Once we accept that love, we are prepared to invite others to join us at the table.

Overcoming the World

Jesus doesn't sugarcoat the difficulties of the journey of discipleship. He tells his followers, "In this world, you will have trouble. But take heart! I have overcome the world" (John 16:33). He braces them for the hardships ahead but also assures them they wouldn't be alone.

One of Jesus' boldest teachings is about the daily challenges of discipleship: "Whoever wants to be my disciple must deny themselves and take up their cross daily and follow me" (Luke 9:23). Following Jesus means a daily commitment to face challenges head-on, but with the knowledge that we are never alone.

When we take our burdens, sins, struggles or challenges to the cross, we turn them over to Jesus, gaining the confidence and strength to be the voice of love in a world of hate. At the cross, we seek:

1. **Forgiveness:** Holding on to the guilt of our past mistakes makes us feel unworthy of God's love. We doubt our "right" to claim Christ's love for others when we can't claim it for ourselves. The cross is the place where Jesus bears the sins of humanity. When we take our own sins to the cross, we hand them over to Jesus, knowing that he has already atoned for them. With that acceptance of forgiveness, Christ clears the path for a fresh start.

   You are worthy. Your past mistakes don't prevent you from claiming God's love for other people. In fact, they enable you to claim God's love for others. You are a living example of the miracle of forgiveness God offers through Christ. Think about it. If God can forgive you, God can forgive anyone!

2. **Relief from our Burdens:** We all carry some sort of burden with us every day. Grief, regret, guilt, depression, loneliness, addiction, trauma, stress, finances. Each of us has something that we carry in our hearts or minds that keeps us from fully living our lives. Leaving those burdens at the cross, means to surrender

our problems, worries, or cares to God. Christ's sacrifice on the cross is not only to cover our sin but to carry our sorrows and pains as well.

Trusting God provides support and relief. Paul writes that Jesus "comforts us in all our trouble so that we can comfort other people who are in every kind of trouble. We offer the same comfort that we ourselves received from God" (2 Corinthians 1:4). Receiving the comfort of Jesus for our burdens frees us to comfort others facing their own burdens.

3. **Confidence:** One of the biggest lies we tell ourselves is that we don't know enough or haven't experienced enough to be a voice for change. You may think, "What will I say when someone challenges my beliefs? Will I be prepared to respond?" When we take our doubts to the cross, we seek wisdom and peace that Jesus promises to those who come to him. Jesus says, "Peace I leave with you. My peace I give you. I give to you not as the world gives. Don't be troubled or afraid" (John 14:27).

We should always seek to learn more, to know more, to have the knowledge to stand on our beliefs. But knowing that God's love is available to ALL people is all we need to get started. Take your doubts to Jesus in prayer and study and you'll find confidence in your words.

4. **Transformation:** The cross is a place that seems like defeat to

much of the world, but is actually complete and total victory. Our own struggles, sins, doubts, and failures can also become points of personal growth and redemption. These defeats are the crosses we bear. When we turn them over to Jesus and accept forgiveness, relief, and wisdom from him, our defeats become our victories. They become the stories that we tell so others can find the same life in Jesus that we find.

Can you imagine it?! The worst thing that has ever happened to you in your life. The worst mistake you've ever made. The biggest doubt you've ever faced. With Christ, each of those becomes your biggest strength. There's someone else out there that is facing those same demons in their life right now. You can be the one to show them a path to redemption through Jesus Christ!

5. **Surrender:** Taking it to the cross helps us get out of our own way. In a spiritual sense, taking our doubts, fears, and burdens to the cross means we surrender our personal desires to live according to God's will. We stop making it all about us. We all have something holding us back from being totally present to God, whether that's pride, self-pity, personal ambition, greed, vanity, or whatever. Jesus calls us to put those things down, pick up the cross, and follow him.

"Taking it to the cross" is a call to engage deeply with the spiritual resources available through faith in Christ so we can see ourselves through the eyes of God. God accepts you as truly worthy, truly accepted, and truly loved. When you begin to see yourself through the eyes of God, the world will begin to see God in you as well.

Christ is the revealer of God. Christ makes visible what was once invisible. When we accept Christ's love for us and live in a way that shows that, we become the revealer of God as well. We make visible what once was invisible.

People are Watching

No pressure, but people are watching you and you don't even know it. They don't need your life to be perfect. But they need you to live into your acceptance of God's love, so that they know they can too. Everyone is looking for answers and reasons to believe in something. Everyone wants to know that God loves them—even if, like Bob, they don't know it yet.

People need something tangible to hold on to—and sometimes that's one another. We have to know we are wrapped in love and acceptance just as we are. Sometimes we are that tangible lesson for others. We are the person that people are looking at to see who God is.

When we know with confidence that we can take our burdens, fears, and doubts to the cross—to Jesus—then we can truly begin to see the world around us through God's eyes. We don't have to worry about what everyone else thinks, because we can live in the knowledge of what God knows about us.

No pressure, but people are watching you and you don't even know it.

There's freedom in that. God knows our past. God knows our secrets. God knows our fears and our doubts. We've turned all of that over to Jesus and can live knowing that God still loves us.

When we see the world through God's eyes, we can stop worrying about our own shortcomings and see the hurt, pain and injustice in the world around us. You may be saying to yourself, "But DeDe, I'm not God. I'm not Jesus. How can I just stop worrying about my life."

God doesn't expect perfection for you to serve in his name. Just to try and reflect God in the best way you can. Strive to show the world God based on God's understanding of you and not the world's understanding of you.

I had to get past protecting myself—my ego, my sensibilities, my appearance—and start to accept the way God saw me. I was so busy worrying about whether other people thought I was too bold as a woman or that as a woman I shouldn't be a pastor. Or that people thought I wasn't pretty enough to be a performer or that I was too pretty to be a pastor. Or that I was too short to play sports or that my hair is purple, or, or, or... We can each compile our own list of the things that prevent us from fully living out who God has called us to be.

Everybody's got an opinion about something. Here's the thing though. What other people think about you is none of your business. If it's going to tear you down or create doubt in your call, you don't need to know. It's time to stop defending *who* you are and to start living into *whose* you are. You are a child of God. Take all of those doubts to the cross and claim that kinship.

Then reflect it back to the world.

We don't have to look the same. Or feel the same. Or think the same to belong to God. God created us to be different on purpose. Some of us got a little spice. Some of us like to get our nerd on. Some of us like to stay in the back of the room and some of us need to be up front.

Whoever you are, you are God's. The only Bible some people read may be your life. It doesn't matter where you are or who you are with, you have the opportunity and honor to show people who God is just by the way you live your life.

Shortly after my mom and dad got married, they were walking to lunch together in downtown Dallas. This would have been in the late 1960s. Dallas was still stinging from the aftermath of John F. Kennedy's assassination there. Unlike today, the skyline of Dallas wasn't particularly inspiring. It was kind of a gray, dreary place. My parents-to-be both worked in office buildings downtown and often met at lunchtime to go to a local cafe.

On this day, they were standing at a corner waiting for the light to turn green so they could cross the street. The Greyhound bus station was just across the street. If you've ever been to Dallas, you know the Greyhound bus station. It's still in the exact spot today.

As they waited, my dad noticed a man jaywalking across the street from the bus station heading directly toward them. As he got closer he started to wave at them and call out my mom's name.

"Miss Merle! Miss Merle!"

As my dad tried to put himself between this man and my mom, she stepped around him and answered the man.

"Yes, I'm Merle."

I wasn't even born yet, but I can picture this scene vividly. My mom would have been perfectly put together in a nice suit, a bow in her hair set up high, and a nice pair of shoes. She would have stepped forward exuding the confidence she had in the knowledge of *whose* she was. Fear wasn't in her vocabulary.

By the time the man stopped in front of them, he was in tears. He said, "Miss Merle, you don't know me. But I know you. A couple of years ago, you sang and you spoke in the prison where I was staying."

My mom was the first woman allowed to do ministry in the men's prison system throughout Texas. So, all through the 60s, part of my mom's ministry was to visit prisons and sing and share about God's love to those men. She brought them a message of hope and redemption through Jesus.

The man continued talking to my mom and said, "Because of your visit that day, I will never go back to prison. I know God's love for me, and I will never go back to the man I was before. I just got off the bus because I'm here to start a new job."

I didn't hear that story from Mom. I heard it from Dad. He didn't tell it to brag on my mom. He told it because it ministered to him. My dad hadn't grown up in the church the way my mom had. So, when he married my Gospel-singing, prison-visiting mom, he was still trying to figure all that out.

On that day, he got it. He witnessed first hand how one person's life can change another person's life through the love of Christ.

Recently, that story took on new meaning to me. Jeff and I were at a Dallas bookstore standing at the checkout counter. As we stood there, and I dug through my purse to find my debit card, I felt the clerk staring at me. When you have purple hair, that's not an unusual experience. People want to know how you get your hair that color or they pull on it to see if it's a wig.

When I looked up, tears had welled up in his eyes and he said, "You don't know me. But I know you. I watch you online on Sunday mornings. I am a gay man and I never believed Jesus could love me. I do now."

We never know when our lives will be the tangible example of Christ's love that erases the hate, the doubt, and the fear from someone else's life.

Yes, that's a big responsibility. You don't have to have it all together. You don't have it all figured out. But when you take your fears, your burdens, and your doubts to the cross you can stop worrying about *who* you are and remember *whose* you are. You can find the confidence to respond to the critics and doubters and suggest that they "Blame it on Jesus."

In the next and final chapter, we will wrap this whole conversation up and claim our place in the legacy Christ created for us.

Chapter 8
BLAME IT ON JESUS

IT'S MONDAY, A DAY I often spend resting in the afterglow of Sunday's worship. It's a time to thank God for all that God is doing through the ministry of our church and to follow up on the many visitors and requests from Sunday morning. Today, I'm also looking ahead with excitement to next Sunday, when some of our worship team will participate in a Gospel Brunch at a bar called the Liquid Zoo. This won't be our first time, and we'll be the only performers there who aren't dressed in drag.

As we come to the end of this book, this may not surprise you. But if you're clutching your pearls, I hope you'll stick with me.

For several years now, we've taken one Sunday each fall to celebrate with a Gospel Brunch at our church, dedicating the entire worship hour to joyous Gospel music and delicious food. It's become a beloved tradition that brings together people from the many worship communities in our church as well as family and friends.

After last year's Gospel Brunch, two of our longtime Crosswalk members, Mervin Custer and Lyn Hinch (aka Cowboy), decided to host their own Gospel Brunch with one of our newest members Bill Linze. Their goal was to help raise money for a church fundraiser we were doing at the time. Their chosen venue? The Liquid Zoo.

Mervin and Cowboy are evangelists at heart. They want everyone they meet to know Jesus. Combine that with their big, beautiful personalities, and you can't help but support them. So, when they asked if I and some of our team would participate in their Gospel Brunch, we said yes.

I had never been to the Liquid Zoo, but I had heard plenty about it from Mervin and Cowboy. They spoke of the people who gathered there—many of whom they included in their prayers and invited to church. The Liquid Zoo had become a sanctuary for those who felt unwelcome elsewhere. The stories they told me were heart-wrenching: people rejected by their families, jobs, and often by their churches, most of whom were part of the LGBTQ+ community.

There's an old saying that hurt people hurt people, but I've learned that hurt people also find other hurt people. The Liquid Zoo is a place where a community of the broken-hearted come together to support and love one another.

Shame on the church if a bar is the only place where hurting people can find solace. But thank God for the Liquid Zoo, where they found a safe place for comfort and acceptance.

We planned for our Gospel Brunch at the Liquid Zoo with anticipation. It's a small place, probably falling into the "dive bar" category, but it was packed wall to wall with people. The stage was small, but the energy was through the roof.

Not everyone knows this about me, but crowds give me anxiety. Being in the middle of one is almost unbearable. Yet, nothing makes you feel safer than being surrounded by a brigade of lesbians creating a safe space in the midst of the chaos.

I found my place and sat to wait for my turn on stage. As I waited, I watched the other performers. It was a profound experience to be in a gay bar, watching drag queens perform Gospel music. If Mama Merle could see me now! The joy they radiated was overwhelming, and I felt deeply that Jesus was present in that place. Yes, in that bar.

After our performance, I was struck by the gratitude from the people in the room—not just in applause, but in heartfelt thanks. Many shared with me their stories of hurt from the church and their families, tales of rejection, shame, and abuse. On one hand, I felt embarrassed and ashamed of how people of faith had treated them. It doesn't matter what we believe; no one should ever feel rejected by God. On the other hand, I felt a great blessing to be welcomed into their community and to be entrusted with their stories.

This is what it means to go to the stranger, like Jesus did. In the places Jesus did.

Fighting Back with Love

The Liquid Zoo Drag Gospel Brunch has since become a quarterly event. As a result, at least 40 Liquid Zoo regulars have visited us at Crosswalk, our modern worship service at Lovers Lane. More than 20 of them have become regular attendees!

The owners of the Liquid Zoo, Gary and Daryl Welborn, were present at the second Gospel Brunch. They were kind and welcoming to me and my team, having heard how much everyone enjoyed the first brunch and wanting to experience it for themselves.

What I learned about Gary and Daryl was that the people at the Liquid Zoo hadn't come together by accident. Gary and Daryl have intentionally created a safe space for this community to develop. Gary is often like the big brother and, when necessary, the disciplinary dad to those who gather there, always with grace and compassion.

Gary and Daryl, had their own stories of hurt and rejection by the church, yet they hadn't rejected God. They had a history of faith and understood what it meant to be faithful, but the church had broken their trust. It wasn't long after that second Gospel Brunch that they came to visit us at Crosswalk. I will truly never forget the day they walked in. Like Randy before them, it took a step of courage for them to walk through our doors. Over the weeks that followed, Gary, Daryl and I had many conversations about their past experience with church and their desire to know God better.

A few months after their first visit to Crosswalk, they made a public commitment to join Lovers Lane United Methodist Church.

This is what it means to fight back with love. Hate will not break us. God calls us to love everyone.

Influence

In today's world, the term "influencer" is everywhere. From social media platforms to marketing campaigns, influencers have become a dominant force in shaping trends, opinions, and behaviors. Their influence is felt in fashion, beauty, fitness, travel, and even faith, social and political activism.

JESUS IS THE ULTIMATE INFLUENCER.

One of the main reasons influencers have become such a big factor in our culture is their authenticity. Unlike traditional celebrities, influencers often present themselves as everyday people, sharing real-life experiences, struggles, and successes. Their content feels relatable to their audience, making their influence more personal and trusted. People feel like they "know" influencers in ways they might not feel connected to actors, athletes, or musicians.

Jesus is the ultimate influencer. When we look back on his life now, we can see how he continues to change the world. Our calendar is based on his life. Our symbols of hope are based on his death and resurrection.

More than 2,000 years after his birth he has 2.4 billion followers because his message of forgiveness, hope, and peace stand the test of time.

Yet, he is relatable. His life began as a baby born in a manger to an unmarried, teenage mother. He was the son of an earthly carpenter and grew to be a tradesman himself. He became a world-changing influence by challenging the norms of the time and through the words he spoke and by the way he lived his life.

Influencers thrive on the concept of social proof—the idea that people are more likely to adopt behaviors or make decisions if they see others, especially those they admire or trust, doing the same.

Each of us has the same potential to influence the world around us every day just by the way we behave and act toward others. No we're not the Son of God, but we do have God on our side! We never know how God will use a simple smile to a stranger, an encouraging word to a friend, or volunteering our time for a good cause to change a life.

When we follow Jesus, Jesus changes our lives. Jesus brings us life, hope and acceptance. And Jesus changes us so we can change others. When we start to live like Jesus, we can influence the world like Jesus.

Dolly said it best: "Being a star just means that you find your own special place, and that you shine where you are." We don't have to have millions of followers like Dolly. Or billions of followers like Jesus. We just have to shine right where we are.

When Clifton Howard came to be the pastor of the church where I was serving at the time, his beautiful wife Barbara came with him. In Pastor Clifton's own words, she was the better half of their relationship.

Miz B, as I liked to call her, was soft spoken. When I saw her, she would often come close, put her hand on my hand or arm, look up at me with a smile, and give me an encouraging word. As often as not, it was a word about our young son Owen, whom she had adopted as a prayer partner. Her father had been named Owen, so she had an immediate connection and affection for our son with the same name.

At other times, I knew there was an issue Miz B wanted to discuss. As always, she would come close, put her hands on my hand or arm, but this time her eyes would look up from under her tilted head with her lips slightly pursed. Quietly, as she patted my hand, she would tell me a topic that needed to be addressed in the choir or within the church.

Even with just a whisper of a voice, Miz B could convey both her love and concern so clearly.

Miz B had a masters degree in Christian education and had dedicated her life to loving children. She worked in churches teaching kids about the love of Jesus. Much of her career she helped establish and run day care programs that made sure every child, regardless of race or financial status, had a safe, clean place to be loved while their parents were at work.

As a strong, African-American woman, Miz B faced her challenges. She told me stories of how she had to fight harder to be taken seriously. She told me stories of churches where people didn't welcome her.

Earlier in her life she had Hodgkins Lymphoma. The disease and the treatment had led to a host of other medical issues, one of which was the damage to a kidney that had to be replaced. Her life was filled with health challenges.

Miz B never discussed her challenges to invoke sympathy. If she shared her past at all, it was to convey strength and to inspire hope to others to do the same in their own times of trouble.

She didn't let her health stop her. She didn't let her life situation stop her. She didn't let what people thought of her stop her. To this day, when I have those moments of doubt, when I wonder whether people think I'm going to hell because of who I love or what I stand for or for what I preach, I often think of Miz B's strength.

I had the privilege of singing at Miz B's funeral a few years ago. It was in the beautiful sanctuary at First United Methodist Church in downtown Fort Worth. The room was filled with every kind of person you could imagine. All races. All ages. All backgrounds.

This tiny woman, with a quiet voice and a strong will, had influenced the life of each person in that room. She didn't need a million followers. She did it the way Jesus did. One person at a time. She loved them. She taught them. She welcomed them. She stood up for them.

Miz Barbara was a special lady. But you're special too. You became special the day God created you, because God created you in God's image. You are fully loved, fully forgiven and fully accepted by God through your relationship with Jesus Christ.

Coming Out

That makes you part of a legacy—a family tree—that began from the time Jesus was born, died and resurrected on the cross. It's been passed down through generation after generation after generation over the past 2,000-plus years.

Now, you know who you are. You are a child of God! You've been called to a life that is bigger than yourself. Did you know that? When you started following Jesus, you answered a call that goes far beyond your own salvation. Actually, your answer to follow Jesus has more to do with everybody else than it does with you.

It's not a part-time gig. It's not a Sunday morning commitment. It's an all day, every day way of being. Don't get me wrong, your relationship with Jesus is not a transactional one. Jesus isn't going to take away your forgiveness or withhold his love because you don't live up to God's expectations.

But it's up to you to help others know who they are too. You may be the person God has put in their life to experience the same forgiveness, love, community, acceptance, confidence you find in knowing Jesus.

Now, you know who you are. You are a child of God!

You may be the person God has put in their life to know they are a child of God too!

Every day, we have a choice to live into that legacy or not. Some days, I feel like I do really well. Many other days, I fail miserably. But I'm committed to getting up and starting all over again the next day.

Blaming Jesus

When I first proposed a song based on the phrase "blame it on Jesus", Randy and Rafe both took a beat and looked at me with a little confusion. After I told them about the article Pastor Stan had written a few years earlier and how his phrase had stuck with me, their heads began to nod and their eyes began to light up.

First, we had to be clear about what the phrase "blame it on Jesus" does not mean. It doesn't have anything to do with blaming Jesus for our misfortunes, for our bad choices, for other people's bad choices, for the weather or for anything else we want to blame Jesus for.

In fact, in many ways, blaming Jesus is just the opposite. It is about responding to the gift of grace God gives us every day through the life of Jesus, and using his life as an example for how to live our own lives. Blaming it on Jesus means we are stepping out of the shadows and into the light to bring awareness, hope, and love to the world in the same way Jesus does.

I'll never forget Randy saying to me, "Sis, this is your coming out song! This is you telling the world you're not hiding any more."

And he was right. For so long, I felt like I wasn't using my voice loudly enough to stand up for the misfits in my life—for the people who the world said didn't fit in. I didn't want to do it any more. The more people I've come to know like Wilson, Mervyn, Cowboy, Gary, Silvia, Daryl, Justin, Veronica, Mike, Jake—the more people God puts in my life who have been rejected in one way or another in the name of Jesus, the more I know I can't stand silently any more.

Can you relate? Do you ever feel that way? Is there someone in your life who needs you to step into the gap and be the voice of awareness, hope, or love because they can't? It's not always easy to do. We worry. What will people say? What will my church say? If I stand up, how will it affect my relationships? How will it affect my job? How will it affect my family?

The one thing we can't blame on Jesus is our desire to stand on the sidelines with our hands at our sides in silence. When Jesus sees hungry people, he feeds them. When Jesus sees sick people, he heals them. When Jesus sees rejected people, he welcomes them. When Jesus sees misunderstood people, he listens to them. When Jesus sees people doing something wrong, he teaches them.

He doesn't pretend not to see them. He doesn't walk past them. He doesn't tell them to go away, clean themselves up and come back later. He welcomes them as they are, right where they are.

Writing this book, writing and recording these new songs with my friends, stepping out of my comfort zone to go places I never expected to be—these are all ways I am trying to better live into the legacy Christ created for me.

And here's the thing. I don't have to do it alone. Jeff is not only my husband and father to our son, but also my partner in ministry (and now co-author). Stan Copeland continues to support me in my growing pastoral ministry. With our Crosswalk worship community, I walk side-by-side with the most loving, welcoming and committed congregation of people I've ever known.

With Randy, Rafe, and our whole music team, we have built a new outreach for ministry in Lovers Lane Worship where we can create new music that shares a message of love and acceptance for ALL people. We are even working on ways we can be a source of inspiration and training for other churches who want to offer the same kind of music and worship to their church.

I could fill this book with the list of people who give me the courage and strength to get up every day and do my best to serve God. God didn't create us to do it alone.

But In the end, it starts with you. You have to find your community. You have to believe that God loves you. You have to know that nothing can change a life like the influence of Jesus Christ. Because today, your life might be the one that shows someone else Jesus.

I know, I know. That's a whole lot of responsibility. But the legacy is yours to carry. If you're ever in doubt, do it like Jesus did:

- Recognize the power of your words. Use them to build people up and never to tear them down.

- Embrace the misfits in your life. Everyone needs a place to be welcome. Be that place for someone else.

- Expect critics. People hate change. Respond with humility, truth and love.

- Pick your battles. Remember where you've been and walk alongside those you face. It's a whole lot easier than trying to drag them along.

- Use love as a weapon. It's the only way to fight hate.

- Shake things up. Don't accept the status-quo as normal any more.

- Take it to the Cross. Accept your imperfections and your fears. Then let God transform them into your strengths.

Yesterday, a young couple, Riley Coherd and Nico Gaskins joined our church. When I first met Riley, she was a young, chubby-cheeked, red-headed girl running up and down the halls of the same church where I'd met Melanie Goodwin. Riley, her mom, dad and brother were active members of the church and her uncle, Todd Allen, was the church youth director.

Shortly after I left that church, the Coherds moved on as well. Over the years since, we've stayed in touch through mutual relationships and at different events. It's been a joy to see Riley and her brother Tyler grow into adulthood, even when the growth spurts were years apart!

When Riley and Nico visited us for the first time a few weeks earlier, they told me some of the challenges they had since coming out for the first time as a gay couple. They faced many of the struggles young gay people do, but feel lucky because most of their family has ultimately accepted their relationship and loves them for who they are.

Riley grew up in a United Methodist Church where she knew she would have been accepted. But the church closest to the place she and Nico now live has recently separated from the United Methodist Church over disagreements about how LGBTQ+ people would be treated in the denomination. This church chose to leave the more inclusive United Methodist Church to join a newly created denomination.

Many couples like Riley and Nico know that churches like this might be outwardly loving and kind to them, but they also wonder whether they will ever feel anything more than tolerated. Riley and Nico wanted to find a church where they knew they would be fully accepted.

Eleven years after a pastor told me my ministry was a mistake, a woman I knew as a child back then joined the church I serve today, because she and her partner knew they would be fully loved and accepted without question.

You never know who's watching. You never know the influence you can have. And you never know how God is working through you to change lives.

Your life matters and people need to see it. You have the privilege of knowing Jesus Christ and having received the free acceptance, forgiveness, and love of God through him.

And if you haven't, contact me! If you're reading this book and someone has told you that you are in any way undeserving of God's love or made you feel like you are not welcome in God's presence, I want to introduce you to the God I know. The God who knows you. The God who knows all of your secrets. The God who knows your past. The God who knows your mistakes. I want to introduce you to the God who loves you anyway!

And should anyone tell either of us that we are mistaken about that, we can tell them to blame it on Jesus.

THANK YOU FOR READING!

We really appreciate all of your feedback,
and we love hearing what you have to say.
Please leave us a helpful review on Amazon
letting us know what you thought of the book.

Thanks so much!!
~ DeDe and Jeff

STAY IN TOUCH!

Join the email list and stay up-to-date
on all of our latest projects.

**Scan the QR code
to sign up or visit
dedejones.org/signup**

ACKNOWLEDGEMENTS

We are deeply grateful for Roger and Sheri Jones, Jeff's parents. Their unwavering strength has been a constant source of inspiration, and the work ethic they've modeled has shaped us in profound ways. They have shown us that hard work and dedication, coupled with love for others, does truly make a difference.

We place deep value on their thoughts and opinions—which is why they were the first to read this book! Their thoughtful feedback and encouragement gave us the confidence to take the final steps to publishing *Blame it on Jesus*.

We are so grateful for all they've taught us, for being the pillars of strength and love in our lives, and for always believing in us.

Rev. Stan Copeland has played an important role in both of our professional ministry careers. It was a long-time dream for us to be able to serve together and Stan made that a reality. And, of course, without Stan's social media post in 2020, the "Blame It Universe" of music and now book, would have never begun.

Just as we began writing this book, Rev. Donna Whitehead was in the final stages of publishing her own book, *I Am Enough.* Watching her go through the process of pulling a book together gave us the confidence to begin our own journey. As always, Donna's passion inspired our own!

Finally, we are so blessed to have Randy Austin and Rafe Grigar as part of our chosen family and incredible partners in music. Working alongside them is always a joy—their creativity, energy, and passion make every project we take on together feel like a true collaboration of hearts and minds. Just being around them reminds us of the difference we can make when we come together with a shared mission.

In ministry and music, we're united by our desire to fight hate with love. We can't wait to see where God leads us next on this journey. We are so thankful for their friendship, inspiration, and unwavering dedication to spreading love.